MARILYN MONROE

A PHOTOGRAPHIC LIFE

Jenna Glatzer

chartwell
books

Quarto

This edition published in 2023 by Chartwell Books,
an imprint of The Quarto Group
142 West 36th Street, 4th Floor
New York, NY 10018 USA
 T (212) 779-4972 F (212) 779-6058
www.Quarto.com

First published as *The Marilyn Monroe Treasures* in 2009 by Metro Books
an imprint of Sterling Publishing
1166 Avenue of the Americas
New York, NY 10036

10 9 8 7 6 5 4 3 2 1

Chartwell titles are also available at discount for retail, wholesale, promotional, and bulk purchase. For details, contact the Special Sales Manager by email at specialsales@quarto.com or by mail at The Quarto Group, Attn: Special Sales Manager, 100 Cummings Center Suite 265D, Beverly, MA 01915, USA.

ISBN: 978-0-7858-4374-0

Design: Kasey Free
Editorial: Meghan Cleary
Photo Research: Lisa Metzger
Production: Leah Finger and Diane Ross

Note: All removable documents and memorabilia are reproductions of original items and are not originals themselves.

Printed in China

frontispiece MARILYN MONROE, CIRCA 1955.
right STRIP FROM A CONTACT SHEET OF PHOTOS TAKEN DURING MARILYN'S LAST INTERVIEW AT HER HOME, 1962.

contents

CHAPTER ONE

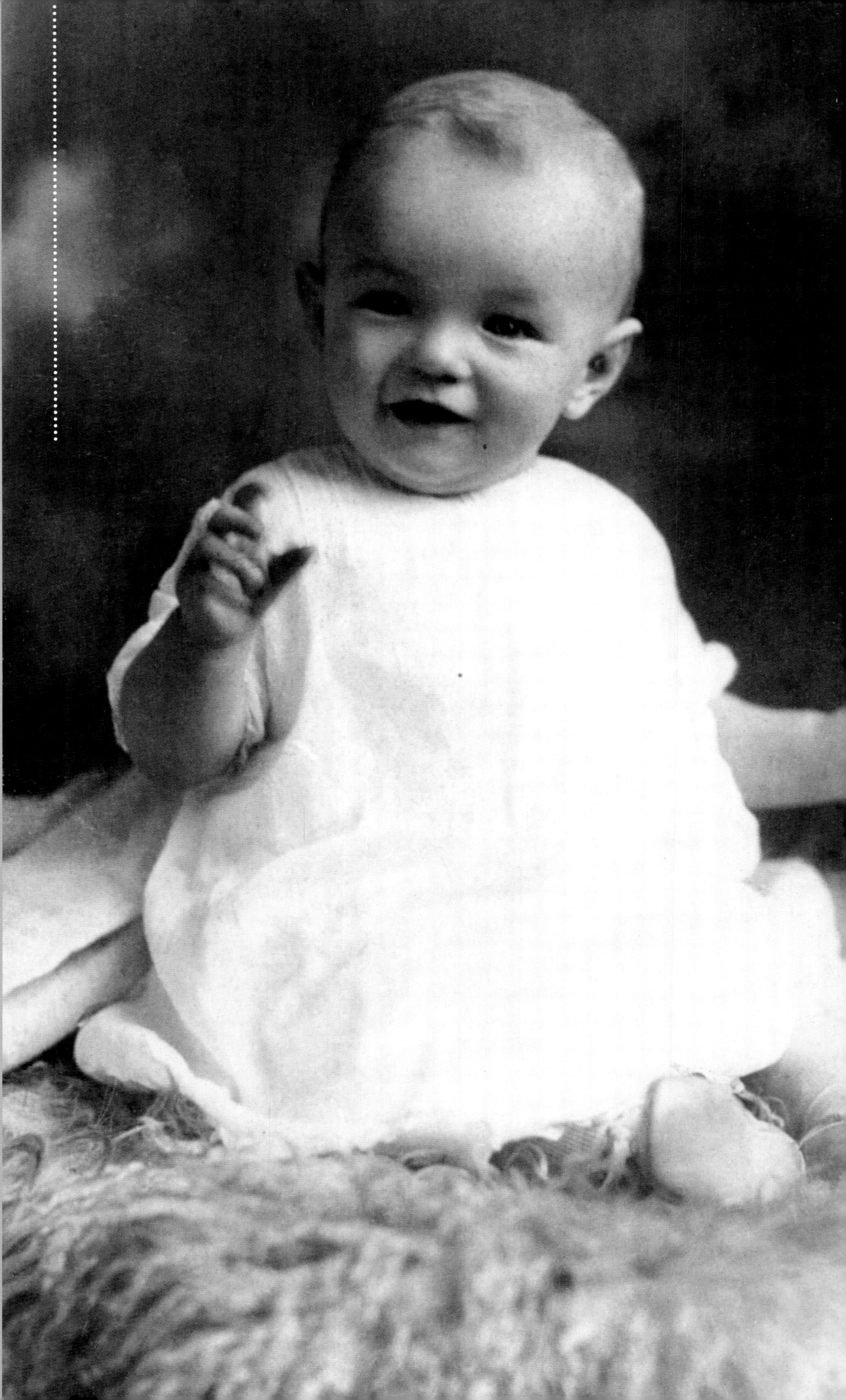

all
TIED UP
within

"I KNEW I BELONGED TO THE PUBLIC AND TO THE WORLD, NOT BECAUSE I WAS TALENTED OR EVEN BEAUTIFUL, BUT BECAUSE I HAD NEVER BELONGED TO ANYTHING OR ANYONE ELSE."

Let's talk straight: Marilyn Monroe was a fibber. It's hard to say such a thing about a woman who is possibly more loved, envied, admired, lusted after, and just plain more famous than anyone else in history. There's no use trying to analyze the whys and hows of her greatness; she simply had the magical ability to magnetize people. It's virtually impossible to watch a Marilyn movie and focus on anyone but Marilyn. Look at the photos of her dressed in black, announcing her divorce from Joe DiMaggio, and tell me you don't want to throw your arms around her and tell her everything's going to be all right.

"I want to love and be loved more than anything else in the world," she once said, and we are happy to oblige.

Here we are, more than sixty years after her death, and people who weren't even alive during Marilyn's lifetime feel protective of her, the damsel every man wanted to rescue and every woman wanted to befriend (or become), when they weren't busy oozing jealousy. She was the world's most sacred kitten: a paradoxical mix of angel and seductress, submission and power. She was full of laughter yet so very sad.

Sympathy was never in short supply around Marilyn. Some of her troubles were her own doing, but there's no doubt she had a tough start to life. Why she or anyone else felt the need to embellish what she actually lived through, though, is hard to understand.

"Once she lived in a drought area with a family of seven people; they all bathed once a

opposite 1927 STUDIO PORTRAIT OF MARILYN MONROE, BORN NORMA JEANE MORTENSON, AT THE AGE OF SIX MONTHS.

from where she had planted herself on the sidewalk. The nine-year-old curly-haired girl was old enough to deduce that she was being abandoned. And "unwanted" was a feeling she'd spend the rest of her life trying to overcome.

Gladys Pearl Monroe wasn't up to the task of motherhood. She was allured by Hollywood, though working as a film cutter may not have been the glamorous life she hoped for. Married for the first time at age fifteen to a twenty-six-year-old man, she seemed to drift through meaningless connections with people and didn't make many friends.

She gave birth to Norma Jeane at the Los Angeles County Hospital's charity ward on June 1, 1926, and registered the baby's last name as Mortenson, which was a slight misspelling of Gladys's second husband Edward's last name (Mortensen). Gladys's coworkers at Consolidated Film Industries knew, however, that Gladys was having an affair with Charles Stanley Gifford, a "ladies' man" who worked as a salesman at the company. Edward and Gladys had split up many months before Norma Jeane was born, and on the birth record, it said his whereabouts were unknown.

At Norma Jeane's baptism, her grandmother thought it was better to change the child's last name to Baker, Gladys's first husband's name, so that Norma Jeane would have the same last name as Gladys's other children. It was never definitively determined who Norma Jeane's biological father was, but she and her mother had no doubt that he was Charles Stanley Gifford, who would cause her much anguish over the years because he wanted no part of her life.

Prior to Norma Jeane's birth, Gladys had already had two children from Jasper Baker, who she claimed were dead; in fact, their father had taken them to Kentucky. For a short time, Gladys followed him to be near the kids, but eventually returned to California and didn't attempt to contact them for years. Baker thought he was the more fit parent, but in reality he was quite neglectful; their son died of kidney failure at age fourteen when he should have been in a hospital's care.

week in the same tub of water, and the 'orphan girl' was always the last one in the tub," reads a *Time* article from May of 1956. The same article claims that her foster parents whipped her and regularly told the six-year-old she was wicked and going to hell. To the press, Marilyn exaggerated her less-than-perfect childhood as just short of a life of slavery.

These kinds of tall tales are all a little eyebrow-raising, especially when you consider that the parts we can generally accept as true are heartbreaking enough. Her mother's best friend, "Aunt" Grace, hadn't told her where they were headed when she packed her into the car to bring her to the orphanage, Marilyn would later say. Without making eye contact, Grace just took the little girl and promised to come back to get her someday. Upon seeing the big, black sign with gold lettering—"Los Angeles Orphans Home"—she screamed and cried and refused to budge. She had to be carried in

above SIXTEEN-YEAR-OLD GLADYS, CIRCA 1918. opposite GLADYS HOLDS HER INFANT DAUGHTER, 1926.

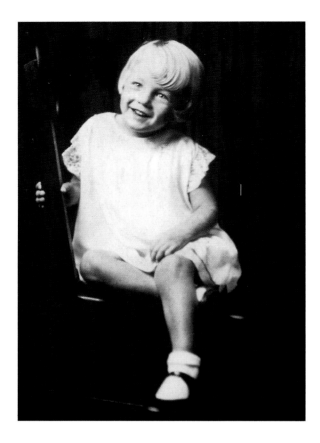

Norma Jeane was her third born, yet Gladys still had no idea how to care for a child, as if she completely lacked maternal instinct. She also had work and love affairs to attend to, and her grasp on sanity was tenuous at best.

Della Monroe Grainger was Norma Jeane's grandmother, and though she cared about the girl, she didn't want to be responsible for her. Considering Della's typical fits of rage, it was probably better for the child that she refused. So just twelve days after Norma Jeane's birth, Gladys hired foster parents: Ida and Albert "Wayne" Bolender. They were Della's neighbors and were known for taking in unwanted children. Briefly, Gladys moved into their house with her daughter, but soon she went back to her own apartment and paid the couple $25 a month to care for the baby.

For approximately the next eight years, the Bolenders were Norma Jeane's main caretakers. They were strict Christian Scientists who tried to rear her with discipline and love, though she later remembered that they were cold to her.

Although she knew they didn't mean harm, she said they brought her up "harshly."

"No one ever told me I was pretty when I was a little girl," she would later say. "All little girls should be told they are pretty, even if they aren't." Norma Jeane mostly saw her mother only on weekends and was understandably confused about the woman's role in her life. When she called Ida Bolender "Mama," as another foster child, Lester, did, she said she was rebuffed and hurt because she didn't understand who her parents were. "The woman who comes here with the red hair, she is your mother," Ida told her. Marilyn said, "To learn that she was my mother was quite a shock. I said, 'But he [Wayne] is my daddy.' 'No, you call him Uncle.' Although they weren't my aunt and uncle, I was only boarding there." The Bolenders later adopted Lester and might have adopted Norma Jeane if given the opportunity, but Gladys didn't offer that. She paid them each month, and that was that.

One bright spot in her life was when Wayne bought her a dog, Tippy, who used to walk with her to school every day and even wait around to play with her at recess. When a neighbor shot the dog because he was in the man's garden, Norma Jeane was inconsolable. "I didn't like the world around me too much. It seemed kind of grim," she said. So she escaped into fantasy worlds. "I loved to play house. You could make your own boundaries, your own situation."

For a brief period, Gladys took Norma Jeane back, and they lived in a house shared with renters. But mental illness crept in under the doorway and quickly swept Gladys away to a rest home, where she was diagnosed with paranoid schizophrenia; she often had delusions that people were coming to harm her.

Mental illness ran rampant through the family. Della had a nervous breakdown when Norma Jeane was two years old, and was admitted to a mental hospital, where she died not long later. Della's father had committed suicide, and so

above FIVE-YEAR-OLD PORTRAIT IN A WOODEN CHAIR, 1931. opposite LESTER BOLENDER AND NORMA JEANE, CIRCA 1930 (top) AND 1932 (bottom).

had Gladys's brother, on his release from a mental hospital. Later, Norma Jeane would be terrified of the possibility that she, too, would become mentally ill.

It was clear that Gladys wasn't going to get well and come bursting through the door with hugs and cupcakes anytime soon, so there needed to be another shift in Norma Jeane's care. Gladys's best friend, "Aunt" Grace McKee, took the girl in for a few months, became her legal guardian, and showed her real affection—though Grace didn't have much of a genuine motherly instinct either. She bought Norma Jeane pretty clothes, took her to the movies, and told her that someday she could be as big a star as Jean Harlow. That sounded good to Norma Jeane, who said that

when she was a child, Jean Harlow was her favorite actress because of her hair. "I dreamed of having golden hair, but instead mine was white. So when she had white hair, I felt close to her. And Clark Gable—I'm sure he won't mind if I say it—I used to always think of him as my father. I pretended he was my father. . . . I never pretended anyone was my mother; I don't know why. I would go in my room and I would act out every part."

Sometimes she would dream about the actors. In one recurring dream, Clark Gable was her father, and he had four other daughters. "When he came home at night, he used to come running over to me—not any of the others, but me—and pick me up high and say, 'Norma Jeane, you

above PLAYING WITH DOGS IN A COUNTRY GARDEN WHILE IN THE BOLENDERS' CARE AT AGE 7, 1933.

are so pretty. You are so pretty!' I used to wake up in the morning smiling, for a little while at least."

Movies were Norma Jeane's favorite escape, and she went to the theater every weekend. She was supposed to be home by sunset, but since she couldn't tell when it got dark while she was in the movie theater, she would watch picture after picture, trying to emulate the glamorous women she admired on the screen: Vivien Leigh, Ginger Rogers, Jean Harlow.

In 1935, when Norma Jeane was nine, Grace married Erwin "Doc" Goddard and sent Norma Jeane to the Los Angeles Orphans Home—temporarily, she promised—for reasons Grace never admitted. Grace was generally a warm and generous person, but she may have wanted privacy with her new husband, or maybe the house was just too small, or she just couldn't afford the girl's upkeep. Whatever Grace's reason for giving her up, the child was now adrift and would remain so through eighteen months at the orphanage.

Norma Jeane recalled staring out of her orphanage dorm window at the RKO Pictures water tower, thinking wistfully about how her mother used to work there. Grace came to visit on a near weekly basis, and Ida Bolender also visited until Grace put a stop to that (she and the superintendent agreed that visits from Ida seemed to upset Norma Jeane). "Some people said, 'It's better that you forget about your mother,'" Norma Jeane remembered. "I said, 'Where is my mother?' They said, 'She's dead.'"

Grace did make good on her promise to eventually take Norma Jeane back, but that arrangement didn't last very long. Some say the reason is because Norma Jeane accused Doc of trying to molest her; others claim that Grace caught him making a pass at her. If either of those scenarios were the case, there was no long-term animosity between Norma Jeane and Doc, as they stayed in close contact for many years. But for now, off she went to other friends' and family members' homes to live as a foster child.

"I had an inferiority complex—still have, sort of," she said in 1951. "When you grow up as an orphan, as I did, when you have to do without many of the things other kids enjoy as a matter of course—including love and affection— you feel a little different from others. I was raised poor, as a ward of the State of California, but mostly I was poor inside me, all tied up within myself."

At one of her many foster homes, the family took in another boarder who sexually assaulted Norma Jeane, she later said publicly. Though she never confirmed her abuser's identity, there was an actor who fit the description who lived in the household for a while. When she told her foster mother what happened, the woman slapped and scolded Norma Jeane for making up stories. Though James Dougherty later said that Marilyn was a virgin when he married her, it's entirely

above NORMA JEANE (RIGHT) WITH TWO YOUNG FRIENDS AND A BIRTHDAY CAKE, 1936.

Los Angeles Orphans Home Society

815 NORTH EL CENTRO AVENUE

HOLLYWOOD 5311

Dec. 6, 1935

Mrs. Grace Mc Kee Goddard,
Hollywood , Calif.,

Dear Mrs. Goddard,-

When Mrs. Bollender was here I told her she should not talk to Norma about her mother .

The physicians have said Mrs. Baker would not get well- that means the child must have first consideration .

Will you please give a letter to each person you want Norma to see and go out with . That would be an extra check . If I just tell the ones who are on duty the names of the ones to see Norma there might be a slip .

Norma is not the same since Mrs. B. visited with her . She doesn't look as happy . When she is naughty she says- " Mrs. Dewey , I wouldn't ever want my Aunt Grace to know I was naughty. " She loves you very much .

I'll do as you request. We want to do all we can to make Norma happy, and to please you.

Sincerely yours

(Mrs) S S Dewey

SSD:MLS.

LETTER FROM MRS. S. SWEENEY
OF THE LOS ANGELES ORPHANAGE
TO GRACE GODDARD, DECEMBER 1935.

possible that she did suffer an assault in her youth that fell short of actual intercourse.

It's always hard to tell where the truth ends and the not-exactly-truth begins with Marilyn's version of her childhood. It's as if she repeated her exaggerations enough times that she started to believe them; her childhood seemed to get sadder and sadder the older she got. Reporters and biographers had differing degrees of what they believed: Cynics made it sound as if she had a charmed life, while wide-eyed others swallowed every tragic anecdote whole.

But why would Marilyn have made up parts of her history? Some say it was all the film studio's idea to invent the stories—just to conjure the public's sympathy for her or to create more fodder for gossip columns—and that she simply backed their version. Some believe she was addicted to pity. Berniece Baker Miracle, her half-sister, has a different take.

Norma Jeane first learned that she had a half-sister when she was twelve and Berniece was nineteen. Berniece was the daughter of Gladys's first husband, Jasper Baker. The two wrote letters back and forth for years before a joyful meeting and lifelong relationship. Later, when Berniece saw that Marilyn's stories didn't much resemble what she knew of the girl's childhood, she figured that Marilyn's motive in altering her history was to protect people. Marilyn rarely spoke about those who were actually there for her in her youth, because she didn't want them to be under media scrutiny as she was, Berniece suggests. She'd give false leads rather than let reporters intrude on the privacy of people she cared about—and she was upset when people who knew her spoke to the press at all, even when the stories weren't bad.

One facet of Norma Jeane's childhood that apparently wasn't an exaggeration, however, was the way her classmates perceived her. Few people got to know her well, in part because she changed schools nearly every year. And she was socially awkward, making it even more of a challenge to be the "new girl."

"I had two periods in my life when I stuttered every time I tried to talk. Naturally shy to begin with, this affliction made me withdraw into myself altogether. I would start to say something and my lips would get fixed into an 'O' shape, a lost feeling would come over me, and I would stand there frozen," she said. "I worried about being left out of things, being passed up by the crowd as a 'goof' and all that. I never could get over how glib the other kids could be, standing around the school yard and rattling away whole streams of merry talk." These kids called her "Norma Jeane, string bean" and made fun of her clothes.

"I have always been clothes-conscious. Back in junior high school, I was painfully so when my entire wardrobe consisted of two hand-me-down navy wool skirts, two identical white cotton blouses, and an old red corduroy jacket," she remembered. "Then, my only thought was that someday I might own, not a big wardrobe, but just enough clothes so other girls wouldn't make fun of me."

In grade school, she had failed a year because of poor grades in arithmetic, but in junior high, she skipped ahead a grade. Her favorite classes were English and literature, and she wrote a paper on Abraham Lincoln that was rated the best in the class. "A little thing, perhaps, but it encouraged me. I didn't feel so dumb anymore," she said.

Once her figure filled out, she had her share of boys following her around, but she knew that most kids thought she had no personality. She told tales of isolation, of sensing that children were looking askance at her because she was from an orphanage.

Donald Pond says that's true. He never knew her, but he was in University High School when she attended. "The closest most of us came to [knowing] her was [all] the talk... that we had an orphan going to Uni-Hi now. In those days, the only orphan most of us knew was Little Orphan Annie from the funny papers," he said.

left PORTRAIT AS A TEENAGER, CIRCA 1940.
opposite NORMA JEANE PLAYFULLY STRIKES A
HITCHHIKING POSE, CIRCA 1941.

A light finally shone in Norma Jeane's life in the form of Ana Lower, Grace's fifty-eight-year-old divorced aunt who took in twelve-year-old Norma Jeane and showered her with love. Grace may have boosted Norma Jeane's confidence by telling her that she had what it took to become a movie star, but Ana really made the girl feel special and at home.

"She changed my whole life," she later told author Maurice Zolotow. "I guess Auntie Ana Lower was the first person in the world I ever really loved and she loved me. She was a wonderful human being. I once wrote a poem about her . . . it was called 'I Love Her.' She never hurt me, not once. She couldn't. She was all kindness and all love."

Norma Jeane never forgot Ana's generosity. Gladys's house and belongings were auctioned off to pay for her own health care, but there was one item of importance to Norma Jeane: a piano that her mother had given her as a gift. Ana bought back the piano for her beloved Norma Jeane, who kept it all her life.

Ana belonged to the Christian Science Church and provided religious lessons for Norma Jeane, who happily followed. For four years, Ana was Norma Jeane's main caretaker, and watched the transformation of this somewhat awkward young girl to a stunning teen who boys followed home from school. Tragically, Ana's health declined, and when she was no longer able to care for Norma Jeane, she sent her back to Grace. Grace and her husband planned to move out of state soon, though, and chose not to bring Norma Jeane with them. As Grace saw it, Norma Jeane had two options: She could either go back to the orphanage or she could get married.

There was a boy who Norma Jeane had started dating while living with the Goddards: James ("Jimmie") Dougherty. He was a neighbor and a good catch. He was twenty-one, a former high school football player with a stable job at an aircraft factory, and was a thoughtful and well-liked person.

above NORMA JEANE (FAR LEFT) WITH HER AUNT ANA (SECOND FROM LEFT) AND FRIENDS, 1938.

HEAD SHOT OF THE TEENAGED NORMA JEANE,
TAKEN IN A PHOTO BOOTH IN THE EARLY 1940S.

McIvor, Beatrice
McMullen, Lorraine
McNeill, Mildred
Mercado, Lupe
Minabe, Hideko

Mirande, Ja
Mitchell, Ja
Mitchell, Po
Mitchell, Ro
Moore, Mari

Morris, Marian
Morrison, Lorna
Nagano, Towru
Nesselroth, Dixie
Noyes, Kenneth

Ormiston, Vi
Owens, Evely
Palmer, Myr
Palmer, War
Park, Jean

Pectol, Nellie
Perry, Helen
Pettit, Richard
Price, Adele
Price, Patsy

Quint, Fried
Rands, Ray
Rasmussen, R
Ray, Don
Rivas, Ramo

Robb, Mary
Robledo, Rafaela
Rodriguez, Jesse
Rogers, Greta
Rubel, Jack

Sale, Betsy
Schloss, Ludw
Schmitz, Carr
Schraeder, M
Schroeder, Je

Schraeder, Nancy
Schultz, Jack
Senecal, Robert
Shedrick, Lynne
Shier, Jerry

Shillock, Har
Shultis, Walla
Small, Eleanc
Spencer, Jack
Stanley, Leon

Stephens, Margaret
Sternau, Bert
Stickney, Frances
Sundby, Dolores
Tapia, Diana

Taylor, Don
Teshiba, Mas
Theis, Marjori
Tillinghast, R
Tuck, Robert

Urich, Dorothy
Viault, Robert
Viault, Harold
Vogel, Mary
Wade, Frances

Walters, Betty
Watkins, Jack
Way, Bettie
Weston, Albe
Wilhelm, Sue

Wright, Marjorie
Wynn, Janice
Yamamoto, Willie
Yotsukura, Fumiko
Zucker, Jerry

SPECIAL

A10

Abston, Barbara
Alanis, Daniel
Alexander, Bill
Alexander, Richard
Allen, Ruth

Amling, Pearl
Anderson, Wa
Anderson, Bob
Apalategue, E
Araishi, Jean

Ariaz, Pasqual
Armer, Bob
Armitage, David
Bacheller, Chuck
Bailey, Bonnie

Baiz, Mary
Baker, Louis
Baker, Norma
Ball, Donald
Ball, Fern

Balmayne, Arline
Barber, Nancy
Bartholic, Marian
Bassett, Violet
Bates, Margaret

Bathrick, Kelle
Beem, Jeannie
Beer, Mary
Beers, Harriet
Bell, Patricia

Benson, Joyce
Bentley, Arthur
Bess, Mary
Beveridge, Barbara
Bigus, Bob

Birkett, Bruce
Blackwell, Jac
Blevens, Virgir
Blondfield, Ca
Boggs, Joan

Boyd, Mary
Bracey, Vanda
Brink, Audrae
Brock, Laura
Brown, Bill

Brown, Dick
Brown, Walter
Browne, Maril
Broyles, Rober
Bruce, Harry

Buell, Bill
Burdick, Mary
Burkhart, Lois
Burney, Al
Burzell, Dick

Campanelli, R
Campbell, Cl
Canty, Ruth
Cardenas, Ma
Carleton, Her

Carr, Elizabeth
Carson, David
Castle, Joan
Chambers, Elizabeth
Chambers, Jim

Champion, Da
Chandler, Jea
Charles, Tim
Christian, Ted
Church, Carlo

Schoolmate Shirley Patterson remembers that, while Norma Jeane kept a low profile in school, everyone remembered James. "He ran for school president, claiming that if he was elected, he would get us a swimming pool," she says. He was elected. "As far as I know, Van Nuys High School still doesn't have a swimming pool!"

James was also an actor, earning several lead roles in school plays. Jane Russell went to Van Nuys High School at that time, and once had the role of James's daughter in a play. Norma Jeane had similar aspirations, but her efforts went unrewarded: "I tried out for several of the school plays, but I was too scared even to do a decent reading," she said. "I never got a part."

The Goddards had asked James to take Norma Jeane to a company Christmas party. Although James thought he was "hot stuff" and Norma Jeane was "just a kid" when he first met her, he felt differently after that date. She was just fifteen, but talked like a twenty-five-year-old. "She was an old soul," he said.

After that, he agreed to drive Norma Jeane to school every day. He had a coupe, and Norma Jeane always sat next to him, acting flirtatious. "Maybe because I was a high school big shot," he said. Pictures of James still adorned the walls of the high school.

Although he felt too young, he gave her situation a bit of thought and agreed to marry her. It was a fast courtship, from first date to wedding in six months. Norma Jeane dropped out of the tenth grade when she got engaged.

Aunt Ana made Norma Jeane's wedding gown, sent the invitations, and was the one to give her away at the small ceremony in a neighbor's backyard. She tried very hard to make it special for Norma Jeane, even including gift suggestions in the invitations. A few classmates attended the wedding on June 19, 1942, just after Norma Jeane's sixteenth birthday, and one of her schoolmates was the maid of honor. Grace and Doc had already moved away and didn't come back for the ceremony, her mother was

not there, and Berniece was not able to make it, but the Bolenders came. All told, there were twenty-five guests, none of whom were actual relatives of Norma Jeane's. Although she didn't say it, it had to be disappointing that so few people who had seen her grow up made the effort to be at her wedding.

For a while, Norma Jeane made a concerted effort to be a traditional wife, keeping the house clean and learning to cook a bit. In James's mind, they were in love and had a happy marriage. They had an adventurous first year of outdoorsy activities. She'd row the boat when they went fishing on Sherwood Lake, and they went on skiing trips together. He taught her how to fire a .22 gun at targets, though she never shot at anything living.

"I'm not the outdoor type and today would say so," she wrote in *Screen Fan*. "But then I attempted to go fishing and hunting like the pal he wanted."

opposite PAGE FROM NORMA JEANE'S 1942 HIGH SCHOOL YEARBOOK. above TEENAGED NORMA JEANE, CIRCA 1941.

left ON THE BEACH AT AVALON, SANTA CATALINA
ISLAND, CIRCA 1943. opposite THE YOUNG COUPLE
TOGETHER ON THEIR WEDDING DAY.

JAMES AND NORMA JEANE DURING A VISIT TO
THE ZOO ON SANTA CATALINA ISLAND, WHERE
JIM SERVED IN THE MERCHANT MARINES.

They played practical jokes on each other and she had fun teasing him when he had to work late. He'd knock on the door and she'd call out, "Bob?" He'd answer, "No." "George?" "No. It's your husband!" Then she'd dissolve into laughter and let him in. He said she quickly figured out her sexual power over him, positioning herself in bed so her breasts would be highlighted just right in the moonlight before asking her new husband if he liked what he saw.

It was only later that Norma Jeane made it sound as if Grace had pushed her into a loveless marriage so she wouldn't feel so guilty about abandoning her again. Norma Jeane claimed she and James had little in common, barely talked, and that she was bored. Despite her denials, those who knew them have said that Norma Jeane did indeed love James. A letter she sent to Grace in 1944 says so outright: "I love him so very much. Honestly, I don't think there's another man out there like him."

It's probable, though, that she became disillusioned when she discovered that he couldn't possibly ever fulfill her ever-present need for more affection, more reassurance, more compliments. A part of her must have fantasized that marriage would be the magic elixir to cure a thousand hurts of abandonment, but no amount of attention from James could really heal those wounds left from her childhood.

For his part, James didn't stay put. He joined the Merchant Marines during World War II in 1943, and Norma Jeane moved in with his family and got a job at Radio Plane Munitions Factory the following April. There, she inspected and packed parachutes, and painted and sprayed chemicals on plane parts to make them more fire resistant. She was diligent, and even received a certificate for excellent work. Love letters from Norma Jeane—sometimes four a day— arrived for her husband, filled with poetry and song lyrics that reminded her of him.

Just as her life seemed to have settled into some stability, though, she realized something problematic: This wasn't the life she wanted at all.

above PLAYING WITH PENGUINS ON CATALINA ISLAND.

CHAPTER TWO

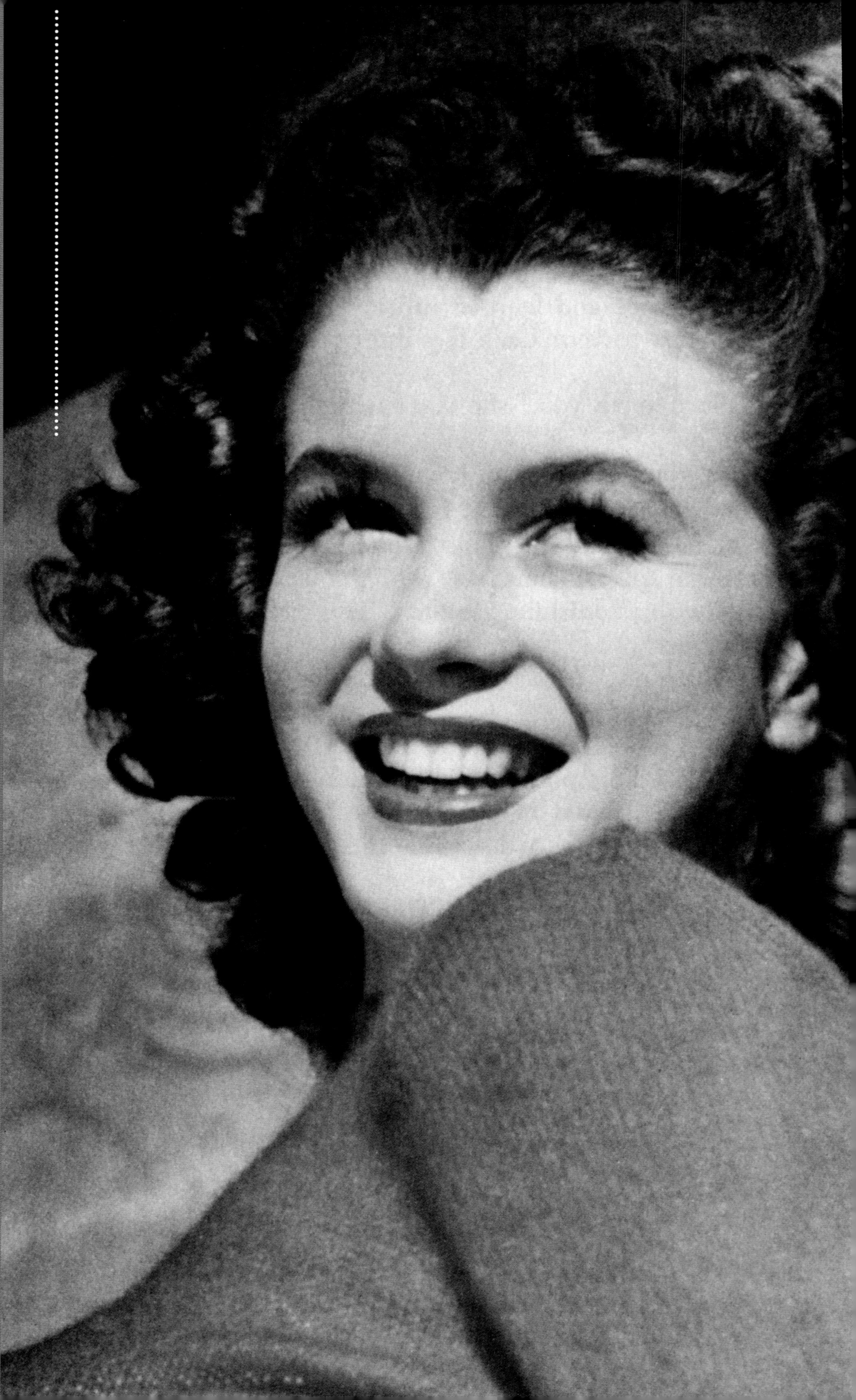

DREAMING
the hardest

"HOLLYWOOD'S A PLACE WHERE THEY'LL PAY YOU A THOUSAND
DOLLARS FOR A KISS, AND FIFTY CENTS FOR YOUR SOUL. I KNOW,
BECAUSE I TURNED DOWN THE FIRST OFFER OFTEN ENOUGH
AND HELD OUT FOR THE FIFTY CENTS."

Dreams of stardom never having left her, Norma Jeane was waiting for an opportunity to make a name for herself—and it arrived as if on cue. An astute U.S. Army photographer, David Conover, showed up on an assignment from *Yank* magazine to take pictures of pretty women helping the war effort. He focused his lens on the sweet-faced Norma Jeane, wearing her drab work uniform. Despite the drudgery around her, she happily smiled for the camera, and turned on a whole new persona in front of the photographer—she transformed from a shy, uncomfortable teen to a photographer's dream model.

It was clear from even that first photo session that Norma Jeane's best talent was not spraying paint on a fuselage. She had a tremendous ability to work the camera, to portray an image that was at once attainable, full of life, and sexy. David told her that she could be a professional model, and she barely hesitated; she quit her job at Radio Plane within a couple of months and began posing for any photographer who asked her—whether or not they could pay her at first.

Then, in August of 1945, Norma Jeane walked into the Blue Book Modeling Agency, which was run by Emmeline Snively. Emmeline was impressed, but wanted the girl to pay $100 to take a three-month modeling course run by the agency. When Norma Jeane indicated that she didn't have the money, Emmeline agreed to let her pay it back from her future earnings as a model—which turned out to be a fine investment. While still in the class, Norma Jeane

opposite ONE OF THE FIRST MODELING SHOTS OF NORMA JEANE, TAKEN BY U.S. ARMY PHOTOGRAPHER DAVID CONOVER DURING HIS 1943 SHOOT FOR *YANK* MAGAZINE.

got a job as a promotional model at an industrial show, and paid back most of the fee immediately.

Emmeline told her to "lower" her smile—she said that there wasn't enough space between Norma Jeane's nose and lips, and that her nose cast odd shadows. Emmeline also told Norma Jeane to get a perm so her tight curls would be more "manageable" and to dye her hair—which had faded from its cornsilk childhood shade to a nondescript light brown—to an unforgettable platinum blond. Sure enough, once she lightened her hair, Norma Jeane began booking like crazy, one magazine after another.

Her first national magazine cover was *Family Circle*, April 26, 1946. That cover was an exceptionally innocent one; most of those that followed were more revealing. Looking back at her early modeling career, she said, "I wanted more than anything in the world for my picture

to be on the cover of the *Ladies' Home Journal*. Instead, I was always on magazine covers with names like *Whiz Bang* and *Peek*."

James Dougherty was proud to tell his shipmates that it was his wife on the covers of those magazines (though they didn't believe him!), but he really wasn't thrilled with the idea of Marilyn working as a model. He didn't like the idea of her posing in bikinis and other revealing clothing, or the thought of photographers flirting with her, or the time she spent away from him when he was on leave. The effect she had on men was obvious. "She was recognized by everybody as being beautiful," he said, adding that he had to very clearly tell a friend that this was *his wife* when he first introduced them.

What made it worse was that in order to get the job at the Blue Book Modeling Agency, Norma Jeane had

above AN EARLY PROFESSIONAL PHOTO OF NORMA JEANE ON THE BEACH AT CASTLE ROCK STATE PARK, CALIFORNIA, 1945. opposite PHOTOGRAPH USED FOR THE COVER OF *FAMILY CIRCLE* IN APRIL 1946.

PORTRAIT BY ANDRE DE DIENES, 1946.

lied to Emmeline, not disclosing that she was a married woman. In photo shoots, she usually had to take off her wedding ring.

Ultimately, the tension between James and Norma Jeane peaked when he came home for Christmas and she decided to go on location with photographer Andre De Dienes instead. James reluctantly agreed to it because they needed the money; she wasn't very good at saving the allotment checks that came in from his work at the Merchant Marine and her income was sporadic at best. But by neglecting to spend Christmas with her husband, she had made her choice clear: Her career came first.

James didn't want her to become an actress either, yet he couldn't talk her out of trying to break into the film world. Emmeline set up a meeting for Norma Jeane at the National Concert Artists' Corporation, where Harry Lipton saw her potential and agreed to represent her. Soon, he was more than an agent to her; he was a friend she could call, sometimes after midnight, when she was feeling lonely. He was someone who lent her money, tried to protect her, and lectured her when she needed it. Once James went back to active duty, one of the things Norma Jeane confided to Harry was that she wanted a divorce.

Maybe it was because their lives were moving in different directions; maybe it was because studios were not eager to hire married actresses (they feared the women would get pregnant and stop working); maybe it was a combination of several factors. In any case, Norma Jeane wanted out of her marriage. The easiest way to accomplish that was for her to establish residency in Las Vegas for a couple of months and file for divorce there. She stayed with a relative of Grace's and went on some dates with a neighbor.

"My marriage didn't make me sad, but it didn't make me happy either," she said. "My husband and I hardly spoke to each other. This wasn't because we were angry. We had nothing to say."

James was at sea when he got the letter from Norma Jeane's lawyer announcing that she wanted a divorce. "I felt like I'd been kicked in the head," he said, although he wasn't entirely surprised—it was clear they had been drifting apart. He told the purser to cut off her allotment in order to let her see that he received her letter. She was in the hospital at the time, having developed trench mouth after getting her wisdom teeth removed.

Before he would sign the divorce papers, James spent a day with her, trying to talk her out of the decision, but although she cried and told him she still wanted to live with him, she was adamant about breaking off the marriage. He gave up and left.

Until the day he died, James would always speak well of Marilyn—or at least of Norma Jeane, who he saw as an entirely different person from the movie star, Marilyn. "She was a sweetheart," he said. "Everybody fell in love with Norma Jeane. I don't think many people liked Marilyn." The woman he knew, he said, was generous and trusting to a fault, always ready to give to anyone who asked for anything.

above NORMA JEANE WEARING ONLY MAGAZINE COVERS FOR A PHOTO SHOOT.

left A BIKINI-CLAD NORMA JEANE POSES
FOR PHOTOGRAPHER RICHARD C. MILLER.
opposite MODELING SHOT TAKEN BY ANDRE
DE DIENES, 1946.

When Norma Jeane came back to Los Angeles from Vegas, she tried once again to live with her mother, who had been conditionally released from the mental institution, and her half-sister, Berniece Baker Miracle. It was an attempt to be the family the sisters had always wanted to be, but they were both disappointed to find that they just didn't connect with their mother in a normal, warm way. She was a cold and argumentative person who didn't like to answer questions about their past. Although it's widely reported that Gladys was soon sent back to the institution, she was actually out in the world for seven years during this period, sometimes living with friends or relatives. She was outright hostile about the idea of her younger daughter being in "pictures." But that didn't slow down Norma Jeane.

Regardless of her mother's opinion, Norma Jeane moved to the Studio Club, a Hollywood hotel affiliated with the YWCA that housed many new and aspiring actors. "I couldn't stand it there; it reminded me of the orphanage," she said. But at least it was affordable.

Harry Lipton was able to talk Twentieth Century-Fox Film Corporation casting director Ben Lyon into meeting his new client in July of 1946. Her first big break had finally arrived.

Later, Ben remembered, "I asked her where she lived, and when she said 'At the Studio Club,' I was impressed because I knew that a girl who looked like that could have the biggest house in Beverly Hills. She could have whatever she wanted because men would give it to her. Therefore, if she lived at the Studio Club, it was because she had character."

Comparing her appeal to Jean Harlow's, Ben arranged a screen test in Technicolor—a rarity then because of the expense involved. He wanted to be sure that she'd come across well enough to impress the head of the studio, Darryl Zanuck, which she did, despite the fact that it was a short, silent test where she had to do little more than walk around and light a cigarette.

Meanwhile, Howard Hughes, the eccentric millionaire head of competing studio RKO Pictures, was in the hospital when he supposedly saw Norma Jeane's picture on the cover of a magazine and promptly told an aide to sign her—or so said Emmeline to the gossip columnists. This was probably an exaggeration of what actually happened. Hughes

above NORMA JEANE (SECOND FROM RIGHT) AT A CHINESE RESTAURANT WITH FAMILY, INCLUDING BERNIECE (FAR LEFT), GLADYS (FRONT CENTER), ANA LOWER (FAR RIGHT), AND HER GUARDIAN GRACE GODDARD (BACK CENTER), CIRCA 1946.

or someone in his office did instruct an aide to ask about Norma Jeane, however, and Emmeline used this tidbit for all its worth, making Norma Jeane seem like the hottest new actress. Emmeline single-handedly transformed this tiny incident into Norma Jeane's first appearance in gossip magazines, just a week after her Fox screen test.

Ben Lyon suggested that Norma Jeane change her name to Marilyn because he liked the actress Marilyn Miller. Norma Jeane chose the last name Monroe because it was her mother's maiden name. The origin of one of the most recognizable names in Hollywood history was that simple, despite the number of fakers who later claimed to have given her the name.

"I've never liked the name Marilyn," she later said. "I've often wished that I had held out that day for Jean Monroe. But I guess it's too late to do anything about it now."

On August 24, 1946, she agreed to a contract that would place her in the employ of Fox at the rate of $75 a week and allow her to take acting lessons with their coaches. She felt

she was finally on the path to stardom that she had envisioned as a child. Of course, her "big break" was just a short-term contract with the stock company—"stock" being the term for the group of young, no-name actors the studios employed. Studios would train these actors, pay them a minimal salary for six months or a year, give them small parts here and there, and see who stood out.

One of the first orders of business was to issue an official studio biography, which Harry Lipton did, making up a "discovery" story for Marilyn that was a total fabrication. The biography said that she had no ambitions to act, but was working as a model. "A short time later Miss Monroe, to add to her income, went to the home of a Twentieth Century-Fox talent scout to sit with the baby. He was so impressed with her beauty that he arranged for her to have a screen test," it says. Several reporters bought it and repeated the story. Studio bios also made her three years younger than she actually was, though it was hardly a novelty for an actress to lie about her age.

above MARILYN MONROE (FAR LEFT) SITTING ON A TABLE NEXT TO JOAN CAULFIELD AT A CASTING TRIAL HELD AT KFI CAMERA CLINIC IN 1947.

After she became a star, she thought back on this first break and sent an autographed photo to Ben Lyon. It said, "You found me, named me, and believed in me when no one else did. My love and thanks forever."

For the first six months of her contract, Fox didn't do much of anything with Marilyn. She took her obligatory drama classes and picked up some new makeup tricks, but didn't appear in any films except as an extra. One such film was *The Shocking Miss Pilgrim*, which some people count as her first movie and some don't. While awaiting a real (speaking) part, Marilyn cozied up to the reporters who worked at the studio and happily posed for multiple publicity shots.

Fox picked up her option for a second six months, though, bumping her salary to $150 a week, and buying her the time to land two small screen appearances.

Dangerous Years was the first role she worked on, though it was her second film to be released. Sol Wurtzel was the producer, and his son Paul was the assistant director. "Fox Studio wanted to get sort of a screen test without making a test," Paul says. "My father had his own company, and they asked him to put her in a scene, and he did."

The whole thing took only about an hour. She came in and did her job and left, says Paul. It was a significant scene for someone with so little experience, and she was playing opposite a much more experienced actor. This might have added to her nerves. When asked if he expected Marilyn to become a big star, Paul said, "No. She was a fairly attractive blond girl who was scared to death."

Film editor Orven Schanzer agrees. "I saw Marilyn for the first time at a studio club dance. She was alone and didn't look particularly good," he says. "The consensus of opinion

was that she would never reach star status. How wrong we were." But he adds that a friend of his dated her at the time and was left with the impression that fame mattered to her more than anything—"As if being a star would bring her the love and affection she had always craved."

But stardom wasn't about to come quickly: Marilyn's next tiny role was a small part in *Scudda Hoo! Scudda Hay!*, a lighthearted romance written and directed by F. Hugh Herbert. After all the editing was complete, she had exactly one line in the film: "Hi, Rad." The rest of her part was cut.

One of the problems that would plague Marilyn's entire career had already begun: She was consistently late. This wasn't a "diva behavior" that she picked up after becoming a big star; it's a characteristic that was present from the start (though it certainly got worse as her career progressed). For *Scudda Hoo! Scudda Hay!*, Herbert didn't mind Marilyn's tardiness too much because her part was small and there were plenty of scenes to film without her. Even then, people realized her lateness had to do with her insecurities. It seemed to take a lot of effort for her to talk herself into showing up, feeling prepared for the cameras. She'd linger for long periods of time in the dressing room.

Diana Herbert, the writer/director's daughter, frequently visited the film's set in the Malibu Mountains. Her father wanted her to stay in school, so he didn't offer her a part in the film, but she got to hang around the lot and sit in on the drama classes with teacher Helena Sorell. During this idle time, she met Marilyn, who she describes as friendly and open, though she noticed that the budding starlet sat quietly and didn't draw attention to herself in the acting classes. The two would walk to classes together and have

above TEMPORARY PARKING PASS FOR TWENTIETH CENTURY FOX, SIGNED BY BEN LYON, 1946. opposite (top) STILL FROM 1948'S *DANGEROUS YEARS*. opposite (bottom) A HOLLYWOOD SCREEN TEST FOR *SCUDDA HOO! SCUDDA HAY!* IN 1947.

lunch in the commissary, and their friendship continued after the film ended.

"Always, always, she was quiet and unassuming," Diana says. "She never made a grand entrance. She never got into her skin. She never got into 'Marilyn Monroe, the star.' She was shy, insecure, just wanted to be liked for herself. She was a very, very endearing and sweet girl who was not flamboyant in the least."

Marilyn's reserved demeanor surprised Diana, because she and her father both expected that this lady was going to make it far. Contrary to Paul Wurtzel's first impression, Diana thought: "If you just saw her, without her even opening her mouth, you knew there was a star aura around her. She was flawless."

Marilyn happily agreed to any promotional appearances the studio requested of her, particularly if it involved taking photos. While she was in Salinas for a jewelry store promo-

tion, growers from the California Artichoke and Vegetable Growers Corporation approached her and asked her to be the first California Artichoke Queen. "No contest, no votes. Pure acclamation," says the current Artichoke Queen. "The local Rotary invited her to lunch, and it was there that Marilyn donned the ribbon and probably gazed upon her first artichoke. Why was she asked? Artichoke growers know a good thing when they see it, or in this case, her."

Looking her best in front of cameras was always important to Marilyn, but she was perpetually short of material possessions. Jewelry, nice clothing, shoes . . . she owned precious little, so she borrowed what she could. Reminiscing later, Marilyn told her friend Ralph L. Roberts that she attended a cocktail party given for the press, and had found a dress in the wardrobe department that she wanted to wear. But the costume designer didn't approve.

opposite (top) ROBERT KARNES, MARILYN MONROE, HUGH HERBERT (BACK), AND LON MCCALLISTER TAKE A BREAK FROM FILMING, *SCUDDA HOO! SCUDDA HAY!*, 1948. opposite (bottom) ROBERT KARNES, MARILYN, AND ACTRESS COLLEEN TOWNSEND (BACK) RUN A SCENE. above MARILYN (SECOND FROM LEFT) NEXT TO DIANA HERBERT AND FRIENDS, 1948.

REHEARSING A SCRIPT WITH ACTING
COACH HELENA SORELL, 1947.

"Now, if you would wear a dress to match your stockings, you'd be a sensation," the designer said.

"I sure would," Marilyn answered. "I'm not wearing any stockings."

But Marilyn was sharp enough to realize that looking good wasn't going to be enough to sustain her career if she aspired to the big screen. Dismayed by her lack of screen time, she said, "It was then I realized that an actress must act." In addition to the training provided at the studio, Marilyn also enrolled in acting classes at the Actors Lab in Hollywood to make sure she was well equipped to be a bona fide actress.

"My illusions didn't have anything to do with being a fine actress," Marilyn said of this time in her career. "I knew how third-rate I was. I could actually feel my lack of talent, as if it were cheap clothes I was wearing inside. But, my God, how I wanted to learn, to change, to improve. I didn't want anything else. Not men, not money, not love, but the ability to act."

As her year with Fox drew to a close, Marilyn realized she was in trouble. Neither of the films she was in had made a splash, and studio head Darryl Zanuck was not impressed with her. Try as she might to impress others, Fox dropped her when her contract again came up for renewal.

Ever hopeful, Marilyn told agent Harry Lipton, "Someday they'll need me."

Marilyn was paying $12 a week to live at the Studio Club with roommate Clarice Evans at the time, but even that became a stretch once steady checks stopped coming from Fox. She began moving from apartment to cheaper apartment and limited herself to two meals a day to make ends meet.

"When I first was signed by Twentieth, I decided that at last I could afford some of the things I always wanted. I began taking dramatic lessons (which was the most sensible investment I have ever made) and I bought a radio-phonograph on the installment plan (which was not)," she said. But as money got tighter, she could no longer afford the payments,

and a man came to repossess the record player, which she said "did everything but fry an egg." She recalled, "I was almost heartbroken as I watched him carry it away."

In the middle of the night, her car disappeared, so she reported it to the police as stolen. Instead, she was informed that it, too, had been repossessed by the finance company. Actually, Harry had made many of the payments on her $1,500 record player and tried desperately to keep her to a budget so she could pay off her debts, but he got fed up with her. "When she has money, she spends it. When she doesn't have money, she spends it anyway," he said. Eventually, Marilyn scraped up enough to get her car back.

As luck would have it, just before Fox ended her contract, Marilyn was a "starlet caddy" for actor John Carroll, husband of Lucille Ryman Carroll, at a publicity golf event. Lucille was the head of the talent department at MGM Studios, and she was immediately drawn to Marilyn—both because she seemed so lost and innocent and because of the potential she saw in her as an actress.

above ACTOR JOHN CARROLL, WHO BECAME A GENEROUS BENEFACTOR TO MARILYN.

Like several other benefactors before and after them, the Carrolls took Marilyn into their home and attempted to help her. They gave her money and clothing and helped her work on her acting and singing skills. Lucille had done this for many young actresses—it was something of a calling for her to nurture developing talent. Unfortunately, Marilyn wasn't the best houseguest—she kept hitting on John, and she became so lonely and needy that she'd call each of them at work several times a day. But they didn't hold it against her; they were so convinced of her talent that they overlooked her problems and signed a personal management contract with her to last from December 1947 to February 1948, and both did all they could to get her in front of the right people.

The Carrolls may have been the ones to introduce Marilyn to Joe Schenck, an executive producer and co-founder of Twentieth Century-Fox who took a strong interest in her. She later denied a romantic relationship, but she spent many nights at his house and lived in a cottage

on his estate in 1949. For Marilyn's birthday, Joe bought her a Chihuahua that she named Josefa. People assumed Marilyn was "Joe's girl."

Joe did a lot of entertaining and loved having beautiful women around for the men he invited. Marilyn understood that she was invited to parties and events mostly as eye candy, but she did what she felt was needed to boost her career. If showing up in a skimpy dress meant that she might catch the eye of someone who could cast her in a movie, she'd show up in the skimpiest dress she could find.

Eventually Joe repaid Marilyn's social favors by asking his friend Harry Cohn at Columbia Pictures to sign her. After she auditioned, Harry offered her a contract in March of 1948 at the rate of $125 a week. Marilyn moved back into the Studio Club, allowing Lucille to pay the first six months' rent so that Marilyn could have her own room.

Marilyn was thrilled with her contract with Columbia Pictures, sure that this was her big opportunity. Just a few days after Marilyn signed the new contract, though, tragedy cast a grim shadow over the happy news: Her beloved "Aunt" Ana Lower died of heart failure. She went to the funeral, brokenhearted over the loss of her closest maternal figure and also because Ana would never find out what a big star she was on her way to becoming someday.

Ana left Marilyn a book about Christian Science with the inscription, "Norma dear, read this book. I do not leave you much except my love, but not even death can diminish that; nor will death ever take me far away from you."

There wasn't much time for Marilyn to mourn; a month later, she played her first sizable role in the low-budget musical *Ladies of the Chorus*. Her drama coach for this film, Natasha Lytess, would wind up working closely with Marilyn for years to come. One-on-one, she also studied with musical director Fred Karger to perform her first two singing and dancing numbers on film: "Every Baby Needs a Da Da Daddy" and "Anyone Can Tell I Love You."

above COLUMBIA PICTURES' MUSICAL DIRECTOR FRED KARGER AT THE PIANO.

Her singing talent was just fine; the only problem was that she fell in love with Fred, who was recently separated from his wife. They began dating, and Marilyn bonded with his mother and sister immediately—but Fred just wasn't serious about her, and she was already talking marriage. For a short while they lived together in his mother's home, along with Fred's daughter, sister, and sister's children. Marilyn bought him a $500 watch she could ill afford that Christmas, and was still paying it off long after he had dumped her. She also had orthodontic work to fix slightly protruding front teeth, at Fred's suggestion.

Fred was one of the few men Marilyn actively pursued in her life, and was quite possibly the first who truly broke her heart. She called him her first true love, and it's rumored that she tried to kill herself when he left her. He married Jane Wyman in 1952, and Marilyn crashed their wedding. Despite their messy breakup, Marilyn stayed close with Fred's mother and sister.

above GETTING A KISS FROM HER CHIHUAHUA, JOSEFA.

left POSING IN A BIKINI ON THE BEACH, 1950.
opposite MODELING A BATHING SUIT ON A
DIVING BOARD, 1949.

In order to get cast in *Ladies of the Chorus*, Marilyn had lied, suggesting that she was a dancer when in fact she had no dance training whatsoever. So she worked harder than anyone to get up to speed. One day, she began rehearsing at 8 a.m. and didn't stop until 10 p.m., despite needing to change to fresh clothes three times. She continued practicing even when she fell and cut her leg so badly that it bled right through her agent's handkerchief.

When the film was released, Marilyn said, "I kept driving past the theater with my name on the marquee. Was I excited! I wished they were using 'Norma Jeane' so that all the kids at the home and schools who never noticed me could see it."

The reviews were less than stellar, though Marilyn got a couple of positive mentions: *Variety* called her musical numbers "nifty" and said she presented "a nice personality"; *Motion Picture Herald* said "She is pretty and, with her pleasing voice and style, she shows promise." It wasn't enough to convince the studio of her talent, however; Columbia had already dropped Marilyn after her six-month contract ended. Harry Cohn complained about her weight and told colleagues, "She can't act." But the decision might have had more to do with her refusal of his advances; she claimed that he had invited her to join him for a weekend on his yacht, and she said she would come only if his wife were there. He told her, "This is your last chance, baby," and when she still refused, he wrote her off.

Marilyn said that she was called to a meeting where the "man in charge" simply told her, "We believe in you and think you'll go far. But at the moment, we have nothing for you at this studio." She said in *Filmland,* "You're not fired twice without good reason, I thought, and if all this kept up, it could get to be a demoralizing habit!"

Dropped by two studios and rapidly going broke, many would-be actresses would have given up, but defeat never crossed Marilyn's mind. She had a single-minded determination: "I used to think as I looked at the Hollywood night, 'There must be thousands of girls sitting alone like me, dreaming of becoming a movie star. But I'm not going to worry about them. I'm dreaming the hardest.'"

opposite MARILYN (CENTER) IN DANCE CLASS, 1949. above MARILYN (FOURTH FROM RIGHT) ON THE SET OF *LADIES OF THE CHORUS*, 1948.

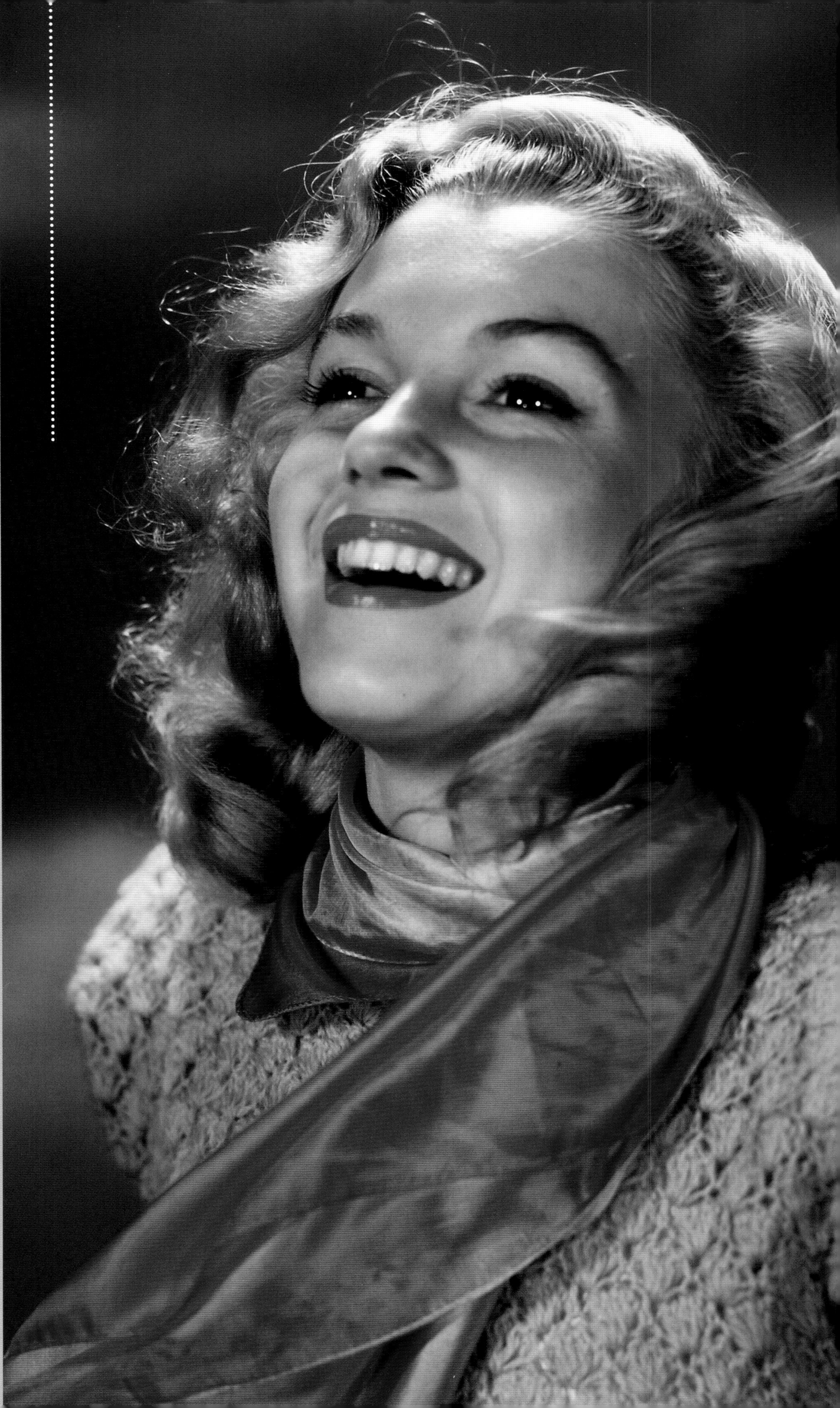

CHAPTER THREE

a bouquet of
BENEFACTORS

"A CAREER IS BORN IN PUBLIC—TALENT IN PRIVACY."

Marilyn already had Joe Schenck, the Carrolls, and Harry Lipton talking her up around town, she would soon add the reddest rose to her collection of benefactors: Johnny Hyde.

They met at a party either in late 1948 or early 1949; Marilyn understood how important it was to be seen at parties that involved people in the entertainment industry, even though she really didn't feel comfortable in social groups. Johnny was the fifty-three-year-old vice president of the prestigious William Morris Agency. He was married with four sons, but that didn't stop him from quickly falling in love with Marilyn and dedicating his life to promoting her. He bought out her contract from Harry Lipton, who conceded that Johnny could do more for her than he could, became her agent, and, according to Marilyn, also became her dearest friend.

"When I first mentioned my acting hopes to Johnny Hyde, he didn't smile. He listened raptly and said, 'Of course you can become an actress!' He was the first person who ever took my ambitions seriously and my gratitude for this alone is endless," she said.

"Johnny not only taught me self-confidence, but he showed me how to make the most of my time. I'd been used to dilly-dallying around when I had no work call. Maybe I'd sleep a little longer. Maybe I'd have a long breakfast. Or I'd make lengthy phone calls to kill time," Marilyn remembered. "Johnny kept advising me to use every moment to better myself.

opposite MODELING PHOTO BY ANDRE DE DIENES, CIRCA 1949.

'Think each situation through. Study!' he said. Suddenly, it no longer seemed an effort to wake up and plunge headlong into work. I found I was less misunderstood when I spoke up and explained myself, instead of avoiding a meeting of the minds."

In early 1949, Marilyn auditioned with Groucho Marx for the movie *Love Happy*, which would be Groucho's last (and probably worst) film with his brothers. "There were three girls there and Groucho had us each walk away from him," she said. "I was the only one he asked to do it twice. Then he whispered in my ear, 'You have the prettiest ass in the business.' I'm sure he meant it in the nicest way." After working with her, Groucho said, "It's amazing. She's Mae West, Theda Bara, and Bo Peep all rolled into one."

Marilyn was onscreen for less than a minute; all there was to her role was the line, "I want you to help me. Some men are following me." Groucho replies, "Really? I can't imagine why!" Then she walks away seductively. But for this short clip, the studio put her on a promotional tour that lasted far longer than the taping of her scene.

All because of that sexy walk, she had a job. "Just like that! Isn't it insane? I always used walking to just get me around," she said in *Screen Fan*.

She earned just $500 total for her part on that film, but another $300 for publicity photos and $100 a week for promotional work. She later claimed, "I didn't get paid until I started to sue."

Meanwhile, the *Love Happy* tour went to New York, and since she had heard it was cold there, all she packed were heavy woolen suits. She had learned her lesson about buying too much clothing—a store manager who had courted her business when she was signed to Columbia was now making her life miserable trying to collect on the debt Marilyn accrued buying a few suits in her shop. "I practically lived on doughnuts and coffee while I was paying for those clothes," she said. When *Love Happy* arrived in New York, the producer kindly sprung for a cotton dress for Marilyn, more appropriate for the mid-summer heat wave than her expensive woolen suits.

Although she became much more budget-conscious after the experiences with finance companies, she never abandoned her lessons. "My salary is not large and I feel I must invest—not in stocks or bonds, but in myself," she said. "I didn't go to college and I think I need as much education as I can get for my work, so I spend a good part of my salary on books; records; dramatic, singing, and dancing lessons. That's my insurance for the future and far better than money in the bank, I think."

The few hundred dollars she made from *Love Happy* wasn't enough to sustain her for long. "Other than a few random fashion jobs, which pay very little on the West Coast, I hadn't worked for nearly a month; I was flat broke, the finance company was after my car, and I was four weeks behind in my rent," she said. "One day, in desperation, I called Tom Kelley, who is one of Hollywood's most artistic photographers, and told him I was willing to pose [nude]

above GROUCHO MARX EMBRACES MARILYN ON THE SET OF *LOVE HAPPY* IN 1949. opposite PLAYING CARDS WITH DON DEFORE ON A TRAIN RIDE TO NEW YORK.

for the calendar job he had been asking me to do, on and off, for several weeks."

Her conditions for the job were that the shoot had to take place at night and with no assistants watching. On May 27, 1949, she allowed Tom to shoot twenty-four frames of her in two different poses. It took half an hour to complete the shoot, and Tom's wife was present. Marilyn called the assignment "professional and proper" and said that the experience was "very simple and . . . drafty." She signed the photographer's release "Mona Monroe" in a small attempt to conceal her identity, then went on with life as usual.

Tom paid her $50 for the photos. In turn, calendar company Western Lithograph paid him $200 for the two shots they bought.

Back in California, Johnny Hyde did everything he could to help Marilyn succeed. He paid for a new wardrobe, minor cosmetic surgery on her chin and nose, and hairdressers to keep her at her blondest. Some of his colleagues thought his romantic feelings for Marilyn clouded his judgment; she was no actress, they were certain. Sexy, sure, but not star material. People thought highly of Johnny, though, and knew this was no passing crush.

"He looked out for her. A good person. He wasn't right for her, which is too bad, because he would've done good for her," says Joshua Greene, son of renowned Hollywood photographer Milton Greene.

Johnny wanted desperately to take care of Marilyn, and because he had a heart condition, he was painfully aware that he might not be physically there to support her for very long. He called her "Baby" and asked her to marry him repeatedly. Each time, she turned him down. He even went so far as to ask Joe Schenck to persuade her to change her mind. Joe took a practical angle, telling Marilyn that she'd have a secure future as Johnny's widow—she'd get his mansion, for one thing. "What have you got to lose?" Joe asked. "Myself," Marilyn answered.

As she confided to friends, she loved Johnny dearly— but not in a romantic sense. His faith in her was a huge gift, and she felt he was genuine, but she couldn't marry a man she wasn't in love with.

On nights when Johnny had to work late, he would ask producer friend A. C. Lyles (who then worked as the head of the publicity department) to "look after Baby" for him. A. C. often took her out to nightclubs or to restaurants, and remembers her as a sweet, insecure woman who was afraid her butt was too big for her to be a star.

Johnny helped his Baby land a role in Fox's musical Western *A Ticket to Tomahawk*, which was filmed in Colorado in the fall of 1949. Marilyn had a small role as Clara, a passenger on the train, one of a group of four women who danced and sang "Oh, What a Forward Young Man You Are." *The New York Times* called the film "surprising good fun," but it did nothing for Marilyn's career.

During filming, the cast and crew participated in a charity softball game to raise money for a hospital. Screenwriter Mary Loos told a reporter, "Marilyn rigged it so her blue jeans slipped and fell to her ankles while running to first base. . . . You can imagine what happened in the bleachers when everyone saw her black lace underwear!"

Diana Herbert, Marilyn's friend from the *Scudda Hoo! Scudda Hay!* set, invited Marilyn to a pool party at her parents' house, and Marilyn accepted. When Diana told her friends that Marilyn Monroe would be there, they gave her a hard time— they didn't believe the budding starlet would show up.

But she did show. Diana says, "I saw her come in quietly through the side gate and walk down the steps to the dressing room. I met her there and I said, 'Do you need anything?' and she said, 'Oh, no, I'll be out in a minute.' So I went back in the pool and we were all frolicking about and Marilyn never came out of the dressing room."

The women went into the house for brunch, and Diana assumed that Marilyn must have sneaked away during that

opposite (top) ACTRESSES MARION MARSHALL, JOYCE MCKENZIE, AND MARILYN MONROE IN *A TICKET TO TOMAHAWK*, 1950.
opposite (bottom) ACTOR DAN DAILEY AMIDST *A TICKET TO TOMAHAWK*'S CHORUS GIRLS, INCLUDING MARILYN (FAR RIGHT).

time, for reasons she never explained. My friends said, 'You're pulling our leg!' I said, 'You saw her.' They said, 'That wasn't Marilyn.' I couldn't live it down."

Lucille called Johnny one day with a film noir script she thought might have just the right role for Marilyn: *The Asphalt Jungle*. John Carroll told *People* magazine in 1987 that he had applied a gentle blackmail to make sure director John Huston would see Marilyn: He threatened to sell Huston's twenty-three racehorses. Apparently, Huston was boarding the horses at the Carrolls' ranch, and owed them $18,000.

Johnny set up an audition, and Marilyn worked with her longtime drama coach, Natasha Lytess, to prepare for it. She asked Huston if she could lie on the floor during her audition, and he agreed. She wasn't satisfied with her first attempt and asked to do it again, but Huston had

already decided to hire her. Although Johnny got her in the door, it was her talent that won her the part. Huston later wrote in his autobiography, "She didn't get the part because of Johnny Hyde. She got the part because she was damned good."

In the film, Marilyn plays Angela Phinlay, the mistress of a corrupt lawyer. It was a small part, but it was the first role she was really proud of. It was also the first movie she was in that was critically acclaimed; in fact, it was nominated for four Academy Awards, and she herself received good reviews. In her only appearance at the event, she even got to present the Oscar for Outstanding Achievement in Sound Recording to Thomas T. Moulton for *All About Eve*. She hoped MGM might offer her a contract, but they didn't.

Even so, the film's success incited Natasha to quit her job at Columbia to dedicate herself to coaching Marilyn full-time. The first time Natasha had seen Marilyn perform, she

above DISCUSSING A SCENE WITH DIRECTOR JOHN HUSTON (LEFT) ON THE SET OF *THE ASPHALT JUNGLE*, 1950.

SHOOTING A SCENE WITH LOUIS CALHERN
FOR *THE ASPHALT JUNGLE*.

ACTING COACH NATASHA LYTESS DIRECTS
MARILYN THROUGH A DRAMA SCHOOL EXERCISE.

hadn't been impressed at all, but now she saw in Marilyn "the burning ambition to be worthwhile, backed by unrelenting sincerity."

Marilyn would become very close with Natasha, taking vacations with her and living with her and her daughter Barbara from time to time. Natasha was in love with Marilyn; whether or not the two had a sexual affair is unclear, but several of Marilyn's friends and acquaintances believed so. Natasha was a rather dark and strange force around film sets, and most directors hated having her around. Starting with *The Asphalt Jungle*, Marilyn looked to Natasha rather than her director for cues; as soon as she finished a take, she'd look for a hand signal from her very picky coach to know whether or not she had done a good job. Marilyn would want to reshoot scenes whenever the hand signal indicated that she hadn't been perfect.

"I want to work toward being a really fine actress," Marilyn said. "Being a good actress won't quite do. I want to be a fine actress, and I'd hate to settle for less. As a matter of fact, and for the record, I won't."

Next came three fairly inconsequential films where Marilyn played three inconsequential roles: a model in a nightclub in the boxing movie *Right Cross*, a secretary in the General Motors–financed industrial film *Hometown Story*, and one of Mickey Rooney's flings in the roller-skating film *The Fireball*. She also filmed a commercial for Union Oil's Royal Triton gasoline: Four men push her car to a gas station because she's run out of gas, as she tells them that her car's name is "Cynthia," the first car she's ever owned. "She's going to have the best care a car ever had. Put Royal Triton in Cynthia's little tummy," she tells the gas station attendant. It wasn't much, but gigs like these kept Marilyn working.

Momentum finally took hold with her next film, however. *All About Eve*, a cutting satire about the New York theater community, would have the staying power to become a classic. It won six Academy Awards, including Best Picture. Although Marilyn's role was a small one, it was important to the story. Her character, Miss Casswell, is unashamed to use her looks to get ahead in the theater world, and she's used as

above SCENE STILL FROM *THE FIREBALL*, SHOWING MARILYN WITH JAMES BROWN (CENTER) AND MICKEY ROONEY (RIGHT), 1950.

a contrast to the main character, Eve (played by Bette Davis), who's much more underhanded about her ambitions.

Johnny Hyde had haunted director and screenwriter Joseph L. Mankiewicz's office until he cast Marilyn in the part, and Joseph said he had no allies in the decision at the time. "I was warned not to select Marilyn Monroe because she was 'too neurotic' and had already shown herself to be undependable. Bette and Marilyn were exact opposites. Bette had perfect confidence, and Marilyn had perfect insecurity," he told Bette Davis biographer Charlotte Chandler in *The Girl Who Walked Home Alone*. But Joseph Mankiewicz thought Marilyn was magical on film, radiating vulnerability "like a mermaid in shark-infested waters."

Bette told Charlotte, "I felt a certain envy for what I assumed was Marilyn's more-than-obvious popularity. *Here* was a girl who didn't know what it was like to be lonely. Then, I noticed how shy she was, and I think now that she was as lonely as I was. Lonelier. It was something I felt, a deep well of loneliness she was trying to fill."

Marilyn's constant lateness was a problem on the set, and her colleagues buzzed about her rudeness, but she still came across on film very well.

Fox studio head Darryl Zanuck finally realized he may have made a mistake in dropping Marilyn in 1947. He brought her in for another screen test, playing a scene opposite actor Richard Conte. The results were good: He offered her a new six-month contract, which Johnny Hyde negotiated for her and she signed on December 10, 1950.

That November, just a month before Marilyn's contract was reinstated, Johnny was hospitalized with a worsening heart condition, and on December 18 he died of a heart attack. His ex-wife, sons, and brother were furious with the woman they blamed for ruining their family and speeding up his death, and they barred Marilyn from Johnny's home. They also tried to exclude her from the memorial services, but she showed up anyway. According to some biographers, she became hysterical, throwing herself on the coffin and screaming his name.

After the service, she went back to Natasha's apartment and left a note on a pillow that said, "I leave my car and my fur stole to Natasha" and a note on her bedroom door that said "Don't let Barbara come in." Natasha rushed in and found Marilyn unconscious, with a mouthful of partially dissolved sleeping pills.

Although Marilyn would later deny that this was a serious suicide attempt, she did say that she thought it was wrong to rescue those who had made the choice to end their lives.

Right after Johnny's death, Marilyn began work on the comedy *As Young as You Feel*, playing a secretary. During filming, she was a mess.

Director Elia Kazan, who was once a client of Johnny's, visited the set and asked to meet Marilyn. He had arrived in Los Angeles with his friend, the famous playwright Arthur Miller, but it was Elia who first captured Marilyn's attention. Elia saw little more than an impressive set of breasts on Marilyn, according to his later recollections,

above MARILYN WITH THE CAST OF *ALL ABOUT EVE*, 1950. opposite PUBLICITY PHOTO FOR *ALL ABOUT EVE*.

hole family to see!
ONSTANCE
ENNETT
MARILYN
MONROE
OU FE
SCREEN PLAY BY
· LAMAR TROTTI 20
LOS

but that was enough to hold his fancy for a while. When he was unable to attend a party, he asked Arthur to take Marilyn instead—which created the opportunity for the two of them to spend time alone together, and the mutual attraction was clear.

They followed up this "date" with a trip to a bookstore, where Arthur found Marilyn's reaction to books of poetry endearing—she moved her lips as she read and kept repeating a line she liked. Arthur was married, though, and quickly left town so he wouldn't be tempted to follow through with his desires.

"I desperately wanted her and decided I must leave tonight, if possible, or I would lose myself here," he wrote in his memoir, *Timebends*. As they parted, he kissed her cheek and she sucked in a surprised breath. "Flying homeward, her scent still on my hands, I knew my innocence was technical merely, and the fact blackened my heart." Marilyn hung a framed photo of Arthur on her wall, perhaps knowing that he'd be back in her life again someday.

It wasn't hard to imagine why Arthur was attracted to Marilyn, but what did she see in him?

"I took her at her own evaluation, which very few people did," Arthur said in a televised interview in 1987. "I thought she was a very serious girl way back and that she was struggling, I thought, because she generally was thought of as being rather light-headed, if not silly. It was because I loved her, so I took that attitude toward her. So the best of her, she thought, was in my eye. Therefore, the hope she had was with me."

Elia continued dating Marilyn despite knowing that she had feelings for Arthur. He advised her about a number of personal matters, including his opinion that she should get away from Natasha. Marilyn did move out—and moved in with Shelley Winters. She remained very tight with Natasha, though, and continued employing her as her acting coach.

Soon thereafter, Natasha also asked for a loan to pay her dental bills, which Marilyn gave her. Marilyn wasn't exactly

swimming in money at this point, so it was a large favor. In fact, money was so tight that between Shelley and Marilyn they had just one good pair of high-heeled shoes: a pair of sexy black heels with straps around the ankles—whoever had a date on a given night got to wear them.

Elia introduced Marilyn to photographer Sam Shaw, who would become one of her regular photographers and closest friends. In 1951, Sam worked on the movie *Viva Zapata!*, which Elia directed. Although Marilyn was signed to Fox at the time, she wasn't working and was short of money. "My dad never learned to drive," said Shaw's son, Larry. "Since Kazan was [Marilyn's] boyfriend, he gave her a job to pick up my dad at the hotel every morning and drive him out to the set. He said he had the most beautiful chauffeur." She also returned Sam Shaw to the hotel at night, and on these drives, they struck up a friendship.

In an almost comic twist, Marilyn "the chauffeur" had a driver of her own at times, too. She continued modeling during this time, piecing together her income in every possible way, and now she had the benefit of a studio driver to

opposite POSING FOR A PHOTO WITH A BILLBOARD PROMOTING HER 1951 FILM, *AS YOUNG AS YOU FEEL*. above DIRECTOR ELIA KAZAN, 1956.

bring her to assignments. It was good publicity for Fox to have their actresses appearing in magazines, so they delivered them to many shoots.

Margaret Kerry, one of the models who worked with Marilyn on assignment, met Marilyn at the Beverly Hills Hotel, where they were both in a group of women posing for a bathing suit layout for a magazine. When Margaret arrived, everyone but Marilyn was in the bungalow getting ready for the shoot.

Soon there came a knock at the door, and one of the models answered it to "this beautiful thing standing there," said Margaret. "She had almost white hair, very kinky, in a big braid down her back, and big, wide eyes. She said, 'Is this the right bungalow?' And we said, 'Sure, come right in!' She said, 'I'm Marilyn,' and I'm telling you, we all fell in love with her on the spot."

A driver from Fox had walked Marilyn to the door, and he told her he'd come back to get her later. Then she settled in among the other models for a few minutes before she realized she had forgotten something. "I have to call Joe!" she said. "What am I going to do? I have to call Joe!"

"Joe who?" one of the models asked.

"Joe Schenck," she said. "I have to call him every day."

She seemed in a panic, and didn't quite know how to reach him—he was in London, and she didn't know what to tell the telephone operator because she hadn't brought the phone number with her. The women tried to comfort her and come up with a plan. It was too late to call London now, anyway, they said; the time difference would mean it was the middle of the night. But Marilyn said it didn't matter: She had promised to call. One of the women thought to call the front desk to track down the driver from Fox, who promised to get in touch with Joe's secretary and have her place the call.

Marilyn was very thankful to the women for their help, and she seemed to relax after that. There were long delays while the photographer set up, so Margaret hung out with Marilyn, and they enjoyed each other's company at the shoot. "I found myself under an umbrella table by the pool and we started chatting about being in the shade. I said I'd never gone out in the sun, really. I'd never been a sunbather. She said, 'I haven't either. It's not good for your skin,' and as girls will do, we started talking." Later, Marilyn told *Pageant* magazine, "Despite its great vogue in California, I don't think sun-tanned skin is any more attractive than white skin, or any healthier, for that matter. I'm personally opposed to a deep tan because I like to feel blonde all over."

When Margaret remembered she had brought her camera with her, she asked Marilyn if she could take a picture of her. Marilyn replied, "Only if I can take a snapshot of you." Margaret agreed, and Marilyn said, "I'll hold off the photographer." They snapped smiling pictures of each other.

Margaret says, "We were all there to further our careers, and we knew she was going to be the featured one, but by the end it didn't bother us. She was so sweet. Not put on, just adorable on every level. I got the feeling with her that what she wanted above all else was to be liked and to fit in, and with the seven girls who were there that day, she was liked, and she fit in. I have happy memories of her, and she took my breath away."

above WITH PHOTOGRAPHER AND CLOSE FRIEND SAM SHAW.

ONE OF MARILYN'S BATHING
SUIT SHOTS FROM 1951.

CHAPTER FOUR

MEANT
to be SEEN

Marilyn took a lot of people's breath away—so many that Darryl Zanuck thought someone was faking the fan mail. An unprecedented number of letters arrived requesting her pinup photos despite the fact that she'd never played a lead role and still had to work side jobs to supplement her acting income. The public hadn't seen much of her, but what they saw, they loved. Her fan mail was even eclipsing Betty Grable's, the long-favored pinup star. When he realized the phenomenon was real, Darryl ordered that Marilyn be cast in any film that called for a sexy, "dumb blonde" type.

And there were plenty of those to go around. Some of the films were pretty good, some were bad, but none have stood the test of time.

During the filming of *Love Nest*, Marilyn had to undress in a scene where her character is not supposed to realize that the star, played by Bill Lundigan, is asleep on the couch. As she stripped, the director yelled, "Cut!"

"Did I do something wrong?" she asked.

The director assured her she was fine, but "Lundigan was peeking."

In large part, it was her body that got her pegged into these roles: People assumed that women could have breasts and butt *or* a brain, but not all three. And as her barely there costumes distracted the actors and crew, they assumed her overdeveloped physique must have been balanced out by an underdeveloped mind.

opposite A SEDUCTIVE PHOTO MARILYN POSED FOR TO GET STUDIO ATTENTION, 1951.

Marilyn was certainly smart enough to know that people thought this about her. She said, "I know that some actresses get by for a while with looks and nothing else. I don't want to be one of them."

At her night acting courses, she once had to improvise a scene, and as she walked up to the stage, men in the class whistled at her. The drama teacher was incensed and took her aside, saying, "You're supposed to be an actress! You should give them no reason to whistle at you like that!" Marilyn was flabbergasted, and indignantly replied, "What's a girl gonna do?"

Her reviews were generally positive, though most reporters seemed to believe that she was just the kind of person she played in those roles, so they didn't credit her talent for acting. But the critics couldn't have been more wrong.

Not a single person who knew Marilyn well reports that she was anything less than intelligent. She lacked formal education, but she was sharp and quick-witted. So many of the amusing quips she became known for over the years were attributed to the studio; people refused to believe that Marilyn was smart enough to think of these funny lines on the spot by herself. It was more believable that she had rehearsed the lines with a publicity flak from Fox—but this just wasn't so.

Marilyn's choice of lovers clearly indicated her value of intellect. Once, she showed Shelley Winters a list of men she wanted to sleep with, and the whole list was filled with older intellectuals, including Charles Laughton (who she called "the sexiest man I've ever seen"), Ernest Hemingway, Clifford Odets, Arthur Miller, and Albert Einstein. According to author Martin Gottfried, Shelley said, "Marilyn, there's no way you can sleep with Albert Einstein. He's the most famous scientist of the century. Besides, he's an old man." Marilyn responded, "That has nothing to do with it. I hear he's very healthy."

To combat her lack of education, Marilyn took a night course at UCLA in "Backgrounds of Literature" in April and May of 1951 with Professor Claire Soule Seay. Because it wasn't for credit toward a degree, there were no grades in the course. She registered under the name Marilyn Monroe, giving her address as the Beverly Carlton Hotel in Beverly Hills. The following year, she also attended the UCLA Junior Prom as a special guest.

In class, she showed up casually dressed and without fancy hair or makeup, and her teacher didn't even realize she was an actress until a classmate brought in a movie magazine on a day when Marilyn was absent. According to school records, she did complete the course, but never took others she had wanted to sign up for; she just got too busy.

Still, she was an avid reader. Whatever people recommended to her, she would read. She may have had few worldly possessions, but she did have her books—heavy tomes of philosophy, science, and poetry. She read and reread some

above RELAXING ON THE SET OF *LOVE NEST*. opposite SHOWING OFF HER PERSONAL COLLECTION OF BOOKS AT HER APARTMENT, CIRCA 1953.

books until she felt she fully understood them. She often brought them with her to film sets, where people would make patronizing comments like "Isn't that an awfully heavy book to use for balancing on your head, honey?"

"I don't mind if people think I'm a dumb blonde," she said, "but I dread the thought of *being* a dumb blonde."

Joshua Logan, who would eventually be one of her directors, wrote in his autobiography, "I found Marilyn to be one of the great talents of all time. . . . She struck me as being a much brighter person than I had ever imagined, and I think that was the first time I learned that intelligence and, yes, brilliance have nothing to do with education."

One of the ways Marilyn proved her sharpness was in the way she was able to shape her own image. She was aware of her strengths and weaknesses and of what advantages she

had to leverage to get to the top. There wasn't much use in trying to persuade Darryl Zanuck of her real talent; instead, she would get others to do the persuading for her—namely, the American public.

She believed it was a simple case of supply and demand— if she could show a demand, Fox would have to supply more Marilyn. Knowing that her body "defied gravity" and that she knew just how to pose to make men go wild, she set out to become the best "cheesecake" model she could be and to make appearances in gossip columns to highlight herself as an up-and-comer.

To accomplish this, she made nice to the reporters and photographers who hung around the sets, talking to them on her breaks instead of chatting with her fellow actors. That made her seem snobby to some actors, but she didn't care—they weren't the ones who would help her get ahead.

above READING IN HER APARTMENT, 1952.

CHEESECAKE PHOTO TAKEN BY PHOTOGRAPHER
BERT REISFELD, CIRCA 1952.

She went on studio-arranged dates with men who were good to "be seen with." She called in tips about herself to gossip columnists. She posed for the sexiest pictures she could as often as she could. It worked.

She racked up an amusing collection of honorary titles from military groups, college fraternities, and publications: "Miss Cheesecake," "Miss Flame Thrower," "The Girl Most Likely to Thaw Alaska," "Miss Morale," "The Present All GIs Would Like to Find in Their Stocking," "Miss Explosive," "The Girl We'd Rather Come Between Us and Our Wives," and many others.

It was at the studio exhibitors' party in 1951 that it became crystal clear where Marilyn's popularity stood. She arrived late as usual, looking like a dark Cinderella in a black strapless gown. *Collier's* magazine described the scene: "While the long-established female stars silently measured her, young Marilyn Monroe, who has logged less than 50 minutes' screen time, stole the show."

Fox president Spyros Skouras had paid her no attention before that point and probably didn't even know who she was, but he was floored when he saw that all the movie theater owners and managers in attendance rushed to her and wanted to know which films she'd appear in next.

According to Marilyn, Spyros turned to the other executives and said, "The exhibitors and public like her, so what picture is she in?" Spyros called Marilyn over to his table to talk. The result was that her six-month contract soon became a seven-year contract starting her at $1,500 per week, and earning her supporting roles in much higher-budget films.

That fall, after filming *Let's Make It Legal*, Marilyn began studying acting with Michael Checkov. She was able to reap the benefits of his direction in her next movie, *Clash by Night*, where she played fish-cannery worker Peggy, a grittier role than she'd ever played. Producer Jerry Wald shared plenty of compliments with *Redbook*: "The shortest distance to stardom is from the screen to the seats in the first row of a movie

theater. She's traveled it—and her background doesn't make any difference. She has inner illumination, temper but not temperament, everything it takes, including a native talent, to be big box office."

However, it's said that the attention Marilyn drew from the male crew—everyone from the executives to the grips—caused some tension. As one film reporter for *Modern Screen* put it, "Quite understandably, this kind of popularity often irritates other women on the set. It would have taken an icepick to break the chill. . . . People on the set considered it a real talky day when the star, Barbara Stanwyck, said much more than 'Good morning' to Marilyn."

Marilyn didn't just irritate women on the set; she often irritated women in general. As one writer for *Motion Picture* put it, Marilyn was so sure women were going to hate her that she "went out of her way to do and say the things that would make it almost impossible for any woman to like her." Likewise, she went out of her way to do and say things that

opposite AT MICHAEL'S CHEESECAKE BAKERY, POSING AS "MISS CHEESECAKE," A TITLE MARILYN HELD FROM 1951 TO 1952. above FILM MAGNATE SPYROS P. SKOURAS BEHIND HIS DESK.

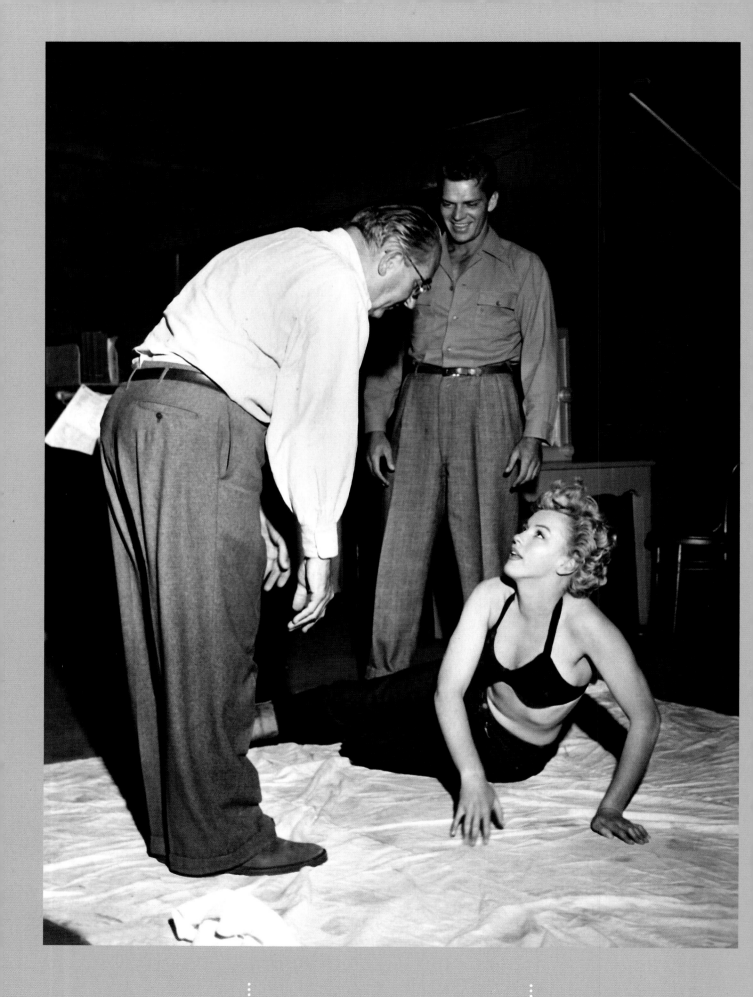

RECEIVING DIRECTION FROM FRITZ
LANG ON THE SET OF *CLASH BY
NIGHT* AT RKO STUDIOS, 1952.

would make men feel she was attainable and attracted to every one of them.

Jerry Wald explained, "Marilyn Monroe was born sexy. When she walks, when she stands up, she's like a snake un-coiling—slow and easy does it. It's natural with her, as it used to be with Lana Turner before they made her into a lady. There's a 'babe' quality about her that makes minds dwell on romance."

Around this time, Marilyn started seeing actor Peter Lawford, whom she'd met in 1950 while filming *A Hometown Story*. When reporters picked up on it, she denied the allegation, saying that they had met a couple of times but weren't dating. That may have been true at the time, but friends of both say they eventually did become lovers.

Once, when Lawford went to pick Marilyn up for a date, two burly men standing outside her apartment stopped him from entering.

"I have a date with her. Ask her. I'm here to pick her up," Peter said.

"No, sorry, we can't," they told him.

Paul Wurtzel, a Fox employee who used to work with Peter, remembers, "So Peter went to a phone—they didn't have cell phones back then—and he called her and said, 'There are two guys outside who won't let me in. What's going on?' She said, 'They work for Howard Hughes. He sent them over to stop anybody from coming in.'" Howard ran RKO Pictures, where Marilyn had just filmed *Clash by Night* through an agreement with Fox. Presumably, Howard Hughes had decided that Marilyn needed some looking after.

While Marilyn had plenty of dates, she clearly wasn't ready to get serious with anyone. "If I were a fellow, I don't think I'd be foolish enough to get serious about a girl like me," she said in *Modern Screen*. "If it isn't one difficulty to overcome it's another, and now it's my work—or rather that I am just at the beginning of my career and so deeply set

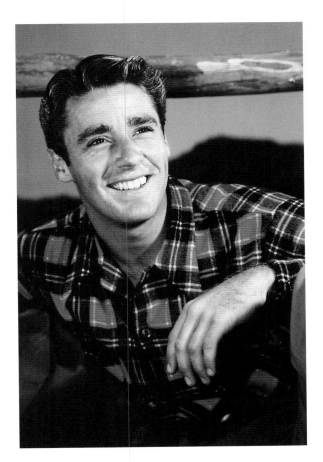

on making good. If there were a boy—where would we find the time to learn to know each other well enough to want to marry? And how could I be sure enough about our future to give up my career for it? Because . . . for the sake of marriage alone, I know I wouldn't."

She wasn't very sure she'd make a good wife for other reasons, too: "There's also my personal carelessness," she said in *Photoplay*. "I come home from the studio, kick off my shoes, and leave them where they fall. I may pick them up later and I may not. I go into the kitchen, fix a hurried meal, and sit on the floor by the fire and listen to records as I eat. When it's time to go to bed, I'm apt to drop my clothes wherever I am. This might not do if I were married."

But she was unafraid to date and have lovers, regardless of what anyone thought. Over the years, the number of men who claimed to have slept with Marilyn grew to preposterous proportions—she would have had no time to work, eat,

above ACTOR PETER LAWFORD, MARILYN'S LOVER FOR A BRIEF TIME, CIRCA 1951.

or sleep if the tales were all true. But those who knew her say that she did have many lovers, regardless of whether she was married or single. "Sex meant nothing to her," says her friend Nancy Bacon. "She didn't even like it—it was just something that she knew men wanted, so she did it to be nice. Her funny way of shaking hands."

Marilyn appears to have had no qualms about her behavior. "I see no reason for worrying about what people think or say about me as long as I can face myself. I owe no apologies to anyone and have no intention of going around making explanations," she wrote in *Photoplay*.

In an article about how to attract a summer romance, she gave her female readers several interesting tips: Never lead on the dance floor, wear clothing of "simple good taste" instead of spending a fortune trying to impress, be "casually polite" to the Big Catch instead of competing for his attention, go places where you can actually participate in the activities instead of just watching—and read the sports pages, at least a little.

She also advises that listening raptly to every word a man says while just nodding and saying little in return is not the best idea. "Incidentally, I think the listening act can be overdone. It is the intelligent reply that keeps the man going, that makes his conversation spark. If he has felt stimulated when with you, he'll be back for more. That old rule of 'Don't let your brains show' ought to be changed for 1951 girls. The modern man wants a girl who is an intelligent, independent human being—without losing her femininity."

But it probably wasn't her intelligent independence that drove men wild about Marilyn's image. Part of what attracted them was the way she frequently talked about nudity and wanting to be bare and natural: "I dress from the feet up," she told a writer for the *Hollywood Reporter*. "I start out nude and then put on my shoes and stockings. I love nude-colored shoes because they make me feel like I'm walking on my toes. I never wear nail polish because there's more of a nude feeling without it. . . . I sleep in the nude, between very thin sheets. And under a down-filled, nude-colored satin comforter—never a blanket."

above TEASING THE CAMERA WEARING ONLY A BATHROBE, CIRCA 1954.

Likewise, she rarely wore bras, and never girdles. "When I wear a girdle, it flattens me out. Can you give me one good reason why I should flatten myself out?"

Marilyn's penchant for nudity almost threatened to kill her budding career. Before *Clash by Night* could be released, the nude calendar photos surfaced.

No one is completely clear on who first broke the news that it was Marilyn in the photos, but it's said that blackmail was involved. Some say that a man approached Marilyn on the street and said, "This ought to be worth quite a bit of money to you. Suppose I showed it around town?" Marilyn responded, "Mister, I'd just adore for you to show it around Hollywood—would you like me to also autograph it for you?" Another story says that a blackmailer began calling her producers at RKO Pictures and demanding money in return for not going to reporters with the news that their actress was offending "public morality." Most contracts at the time had a clause that guaranteed that their actors

wouldn't do anything immoral—posing nude was certainly on that list in 1951.

The photographer had sold the rights for the two best shots to John Baumgarth's calendar company, Western Lithograph, for a flat fee, and the first was printed in 1951's calendar. The shot was titled "A New Wrinkle," showing Marilyn stretched out across red velvet. The second shot, where Marilyn is seated, proved the more popular over time. In fact, the very first issue of *Playboy* featured this shot as a centerfold and a clothed Marilyn on the cover.

As columnist Hedda Hopper wrote about the calendars in 1953, "The company bought two for $200—a small fee for Kelley's work, but better than nothing. The calendars were printed and sold slowly. For almost two years they were shipped out with the other regulars and nobody thought much about it. Then one day an executive of the company came running into the office looking as though he was about to have a stroke. 'I went to the movies last night,' he stuttered, 'and I think that blonde dame on one of our calendars is Marilyn Monroe.'"

above ONE OF THE INFAMOUS NUDE PHOTOGRAPHS, "A NEW WRINKLE," TAKEN BY TOM KELLEY IN 1949 AND RELEASED ON A 1951 WALL CALENDAR.

TOM KELLEY'S OTHER NUDE SHOT OF
MARILYN, FEATURED AS THE CENTERFOLD
IN *PLAYBOY*'S FIRST ISSUE.

Someone tipped off Aline Mosby, a Hollywood reporter for United Press International. In 1991 she claimed, "I can't remember who tipped me off to that . . . I remember going to the calendar company and they confirmed it."

In an article she wrote for *Collier's* magazine in 1956, Aline wrote that she first interviewed Marilyn about the sensation she caused wearing revealing dresses. "Then I put my pencil away and asked about that nude calendar the Hollywood grapevine whispered she had posed for. Marilyn, erroneously thinking she no longer was talking for print, confessed all in her wonderful breathless voice. (Later she told me that after the first horrified gulp she was glad the story finally was officially printed because 'some people thought the calendar was bad or something.')"

In fact, Marilyn was a savvy woman who knew just what she was doing with her image and career. She had already planned how she would handle it when this story broke—just as she expected it would. She had even talked it over with people at the studio and with her friends, who were split about what they wanted her to do: Some wanted her to lie about it (or at least not confirm the rumor), and others said she should go ahead and be honest about it. She preferred the latter approach, and wanted to get across that she was not ashamed for having done it.

Tom Kelley suggests that it was Marilyn herself who tipped off reporters. After the calendar was printed, she called Tom and asked for twenty-five copies. "All I know is that as soon as Marilyn received the twenty-five copies, she passed them out to some friends on the set, including a few photographers and newsmen. She was plenty smart and knew her stuff," he wrote.

But when Aline called and let Fox executives know that she had discovered the calendar, Zanuck was furious with Marilyn, and called an emergency meeting with Harry Brand to figure out what to do. She should be fired! She should be boiled in oil! In the end, they agreed that Marilyn could

confirm the story as long as she played up the fact that she was really down on her luck at the time.

The story hit the press on March 13, and public sentiment was nearly uniformly sympathetic. There were no giant protests, no angry people storming the studio. In fact, it seemed that people kind of admired her for being so unashamed of her body and her sexuality. So contrary to Zanuck's fears, the "scandal" didn't hurt Marilyn's reviews at all. When *Clash by Night* came out in May, the *New York World-Telegram & Sun* reviewer wrote that Marilyn was "a forceful actress, a gifted new star, worthy of all that fantastic press agentry. Her role here is not very big, but she makes it dominant."

"The body is meant to be seen, not all covered up," she once said. When reporters asked if she was really nude for the shoot, she said, "It's not true that I had nothing on. I had the radio on." It was an interesting time in America's social history: Marilyn was right on the cusp of a change between the more puritanical fifties and the "free love" sixties, and she very well may have tipped the scale.

above THE COVER OF *PLAYBOY*'S FIRST ISSUE, DECEMBER 1953.

MEANT TO BE SEEN

CHAPTER FIVE

BASES
loaded

"THE TROUBLE WITH CENSORS IS THAT THEY WORRY IF A GIRL HAS CLEAVAGE. THEY OUGHT TO WORRY IF SHE HASN'T ANY."

In 1951, Fox press agents set up a publicity shoot for Marilyn with the Chicago White Sox during spring training. They grabbed tall, handsome baseball player Gus Zernial to pose with her, along with Joe Dobson. They pretended to help her learn a proper batting stance and practice her swing. The press loved it, but baseball legend Joe DiMaggio didn't. He was jealous.

"He couldn't believe someone like me could meet Marilyn Monroe. He made the comment, 'Why should a busher like [you] get to meet her?'" said Gus in a 2006 issue of *Baseball Digest*. Joe asked Gus how he could contact the beautiful blonde, and Gus gave him Marilyn's publicist's information.

"I introduced Joe to Marilyn indirectly through the photo shoot," Gus said, but apparently some gossip columnists ran with an exaggerated version of Gus's role, making it sound as if Gus knew Marilyn and had set the pair up. Joe got angry because he believed that Gus had told that to reporters. "Joe stayed mad at me the whole time he was alive."

"I can understand why Joe fell in love with her at first sight," Gus told a *Telegraph* reporter. "I fell in love with her at first sight. She was gorgeous and much more intelligent than people might think."

Intent on meeting her and used to getting his way, Joe set up a double date through mutual acquaintance David Marsh, who saw the opportunity for a terrific publicity coup.

opposite MARILYN IN 1951.

David brought along another actress, and they all waited at the Villa Nova Restaurant on March 8, 1952, for Marilyn's arrival. But after an hour, when she hadn't shown, David called her—and she tried to back out.

"Please, I'm tired," she said. Athletes just weren't her type. She'd never even been to a baseball game. "I don't like men in loud clothes, with checked suits, and big muscles, and pink ties. I get nervous," she told him.

David explained that Joe was nothing like that, and that she had better show up because they were waiting around for her, and it would be good for her career.

But she was past "career dating," she thought. A few months earlier, she had said, "Sometimes, the studio would suggest that I go out with someone, when I didn't care if I was seen at such-and-such a place, with such-and-such a person! After a while, they understood and stopped suggesting it." Two hours late when she finally arrived, she didn't know what to make of the quiet man sitting next to her. Rather than fall into uncomfortable silence, she mostly chatted with David about the movie she was working on (*Monkey Business*), until actor Mickey Rooney interrupted their conversation when he rushed across the room to greet Joe.

Mickey's reaction to Joe impressed Marilyn. Here was a famous actor falling all over himself to talk to her date. "Then I became aware of something odd," she says in *My Story*, the autobiography ghostwritten by Ben Hecht. "The men at the table weren't showing off for me or telling their stories for my attention. It was Mr. DiMaggio they were wooing. This was a novelty. No woman has ever put me so much in the shade before."

What she liked so much about Joe was his coolness. He came across as undramatic, serious, and even a bit shy. By the end of the night, she knew she wanted to spend time alone with him, so she offered him a ride—and spent the next three hours in his company. Afterward, he called her every day, and they went out every night while he was in town; within a few months, he brought her home to meet his family.

"I'm sure that almost every girl believes in her inner heart that the most important thing in life is to have a man love her. One man," she wrote in *Photoplay*.

Joe was crazy about her from the start, but like James Dougherty, he was not at all crazy about her Hollywood lifestyle. He was newly retired from baseball and had never much liked the limelight to begin with—at least, not the type of limelight Marilyn was standing in. The sycophants, the parties, the publicity photos . . . these weren't Joe's style.

The fact is that Marilyn didn't necessarily enjoy every part of fame either, but she kept doing whatever she thought would benefit her career. And while she tried to ignore it, she did realize that a majority of the people she considered her friends were on her payroll in one way or another.

"People expect to find me one of two things," she said to a *Parade* writer in 1952. "Either a tart or a dumb blonde. *I'm neither.* The fact is that I'm lonely—in spite of the fastest ride to popularity that any girl ever had. Too much publicity

opposite WITH JOE DOBSON, EDWARD ERAUTT, AND GUS ZERNIAL OF THE CHICAGO WHITE SOX DURING A 1951 PUBLICITY SHOOT. above NEW YORK YANKEES SLUGGER JOE DIMAGGIO.

makes you lonely. Suddenly you see people speaking to you and being nice to you. But they never did before, and you feel it's happening only because you're now a 'personality.' And with me, I know, it would have meant a lot more to have had a few words of encouragement before—when I really needed them."

Somehow, Joe withstood the nude calendar photo episode, which happened the same month they met. Close on the heels of that issue came a second publicity problem: Someone discovered that Marilyn wasn't an orphan despite what her studio biographies claimed and despite what she had long reported in interviews.

Hollywood reporter Erskine Johnson had tracked down Gladys in the mental institution, requiring Marilyn to do

some serious explaining of her past. But once again, what could have been a career-killing nightmare was just a minor blip, another episode that may have even garnered more sympathy for her.

She was in the hospital recovering from an appendectomy when the news broke, and she explained herself in a way that most found difficult to criticize. She said that she had never really known her mother or had a normal relationship with her, and that she claimed to be an orphan to keep the poor woman out of the spotlight.

Maybe it was more heartbreaking for people to realize that Marilyn did have a mother who was institutionalized and had never truly been a figure in her life, than to believe she was an orphan. All was forgiven.

above MARILYN AND JOE OUT ON THE TOWN DURING THEIR COURTSHIP, 1953.

RECOVERING WELL AFTER HER
APPENDECTOMY, MAY 1952.

WITH DONNA CORCORAN (LEFT) ON THE
SET OF *DON'T BOTHER TO KNOCK*.

A little less kind, though, were her reviews for *Don't Bother to Knock*. The film was a first for Marilyn in two ways: It was her first lead role and her first dramatic role—both things she had been working hard to achieve. In the film, she plays psychotic babysitter Nell Forbes. A few reviews were complimentary, such as the *New York Daily Mirror*, which called her "more than a sexy dame. She has good dramatic promise." But more of them didn't exactly know what to make of Marilyn or the film, such as the *New York Post*'s claim that "they've thrown Marilyn Monroe into the deep dramatic waters, sink or swim, and while she doesn't really do either, you might say that she floats. With that figure, what else can she do?"

To the *Parade* writer, Marilyn admitted that all the publicity was setting her on edge: "I'm beginning to feel like a piece of statuary that people are inspecting with a magnifying glass, looking for imperfections—taking apart my dress, my voice, my figure, my acting—everything about me. When you're an obscure bit player or starlet, nobody cares whether you can act. But when your name is up in lights, it's different. I do a picture like *Don't Bother to Knock* and some people say, 'Leave the dramatics to Bette Davis and Olivia de Havilland. Keep Marilyn Monroe in a tight dress and let her drip sex.' It kind of gets me."

Despite the criticisms, Marilyn was still pretty trusting of people at this point. That would slowly change throughout her life, as she became more and more cynical about being used. But for now, those who knew her describe her as "wide-eyed."

"She was very naïve. I don't understand how she could be that naïve with all the things that happened to her in life, but she was," says friend Nancy Bacon. "Anybody could tell her to do anything, and she would do it."

One friend of theirs, writer Jim Henaghan, was entertaining some wealthy acquaintances late one night when the talk turned to his friendship with Marilyn. They had been

drinking, and he suggested, "I could get Marilyn Monroe to show you her appendix scar."

"Yeah, right, a thousand bucks says you won't," one of the guys said.

So Jim took them to the Beverly Hills Hotel, where Marilyn was staying.

"Marilyn, show these guys your appendix scar," he said . . . and she promptly pulled down her pajamas and showed them, no questions asked.

Marilyn's next film to shoot was *Niagara*, another major milestone in her career. She received top billing, and the film was given the tagline "Marilyn Monroe and 'Niagara': a raging torrent of emotion that even nature can't control!"

"We had a wonderful time up at the Falls doing that," actor Max Showalter (who played Ray Cutler) told Robert L. Smith of *Videoscope* magazine. "Marilyn was usually late, but whenever she did come on the set, you were really focused right on Marilyn. Sometimes it would take a lot of takes.

above ORIGINAL MOVIE POSTER FOR *NIAGARA*, 1953.

Coming from the theater, I always felt the first take was the best take, but we'd have to go along with Marilyn. By the time she got it right, she was perfect and the rest of us were worn out!"

Reviews were good, and the box office results were better. Marilyn managed to "be in a tight dress and drip sex" while also playing a meaty role. It was official: Marilyn had shed her starlet skin to become a real star.

The year 1952 was filled with all sorts of career milestones, personal changes, and publicity appearances. She was chosen as the grand marshal of the Miss America pageant that September and was asked to pose for photos with women in the armed forces. However, an army representative tried to bar some of the photos from being published because Marilyn's dress was low-cut and the photographer was purposely shooting downward at her to emphasize her cleavage. He didn't want the army women associated with

such a thing—which, of course, made it all the more delicious to the press when they found out about the shoot.

Reporters have always said that Marilyn quipped that although she noticed people checking her out that day, "I thought people were looking at my grand marshal's badge." It did sound perfectly Marilyn-esque, but she never said such a thing. She was growing increasingly frustrated by the liberties reporters would take in inventing quotes and stories about her.

Joe visited her on her film sets, but it's hard to know if he was mostly there to see her or to intimidate others. Her friends were often put off by him, seeing him as cold and unfriendly. At least one director would wind up barring him from set because of the way he unnerved people by staring them down, making it clear that he disapproved of the industry in general, and specifically of anyone who looked at Marilyn.

above MARILYN AS GRAND MARSHAL AT THE 1952 MISS AMERICA PAGEANT.

He particularly disliked acting coach Natasha, who disliked him right back. If she called Marilyn and he answered the phone, he'd tell her to call Marilyn's agent if she had anything to communicate with his girlfriend.

Meanwhile, Marilyn was just trying to figure out where she really stood. "I want to find myself way deep inside, and enjoy being myself," she told a *Coronet* reporter. "It isn't easy. Nothing's ever easy as long as you go on living."

In May of 1952, Joe's ex-wife, Dorothy Arnold, saw a picture in the newspaper of her son with Joe and Marilyn at the Bel Air Hotel pool—and she got upset. Joe Jr. was ten at the time, and he told his mother that Joe Sr. called Marilyn "doll" and talked about her beautiful legs. Dorothy tried to get the courts to keep Marilyn away from Joe Jr., saying that the woman was a threat to the boy's morals.

Reporters from *Movie Star Parade* responded to Dorothy's motion by writing that they had seen the threesome at the pool, and "We would like to go on record as saying that she is the most considerate 'stepmother' we know. The boy seemed to be in seventh heaven as Marilyn waited on him hand and foot, making every effort to satisfy his every whim. There was ice cream and cake galore and Marilyn never got more than six feet away from the lad when he was in the water. In our opinion she was a perfect lifeguard—because no matter where she went, there were no less than eleven husky guys standing by to save anybody at the crook of her little finger."

Dorothy's suit was dropped in 1953. Instead, she asked the courts to rule that Joe and Marilyn could not take Joe Jr. out in places where there was drinking or where there were no other youngsters.

Joe Jr. and Marilyn had a good relationship all through her life. While she and Joe Sr. were dating, she was even involved at Joe Jr.'s school, the Black-Foxe Military Academy, a prestigious institution filled with children of celebrities. "Every Friday there would be a parade in the drill field," says children's author Daniel Pinkwater, who was a student with Joe Jr. He remembers Joe as one of the nicest, most popular kids at the academy. "We'd take out our little rifles, and they would march us around, the band would play, and the parents would come collect their kids and take them home for the weekend . . . or in some cases, take them out for a milkshake and bring them back to school an hour later. Some kids never went home.

"Joe and Marilyn would be there in the crowd of people standing at the parade ground watching us pass. I remember her with bare arms and shoulders, spilling out of the top of her top. She had to stand still for about twenty minutes, the sun shining on her golden hair and her creamy skin. Then at the end of the exercise, she would squat and extend her arms out to the side and holler in a very loud, clear voice, 'Joeeeeeeey, come to Marilyn!' and the kid would die. We'd all die in sympathy. The high school boys were dying in a different way."

above JOE DIMAGGIO JR. WITH HIS FATHER AFTER THE WORLD SERIES, OCTOBER 1953.

CHAPTER SIX

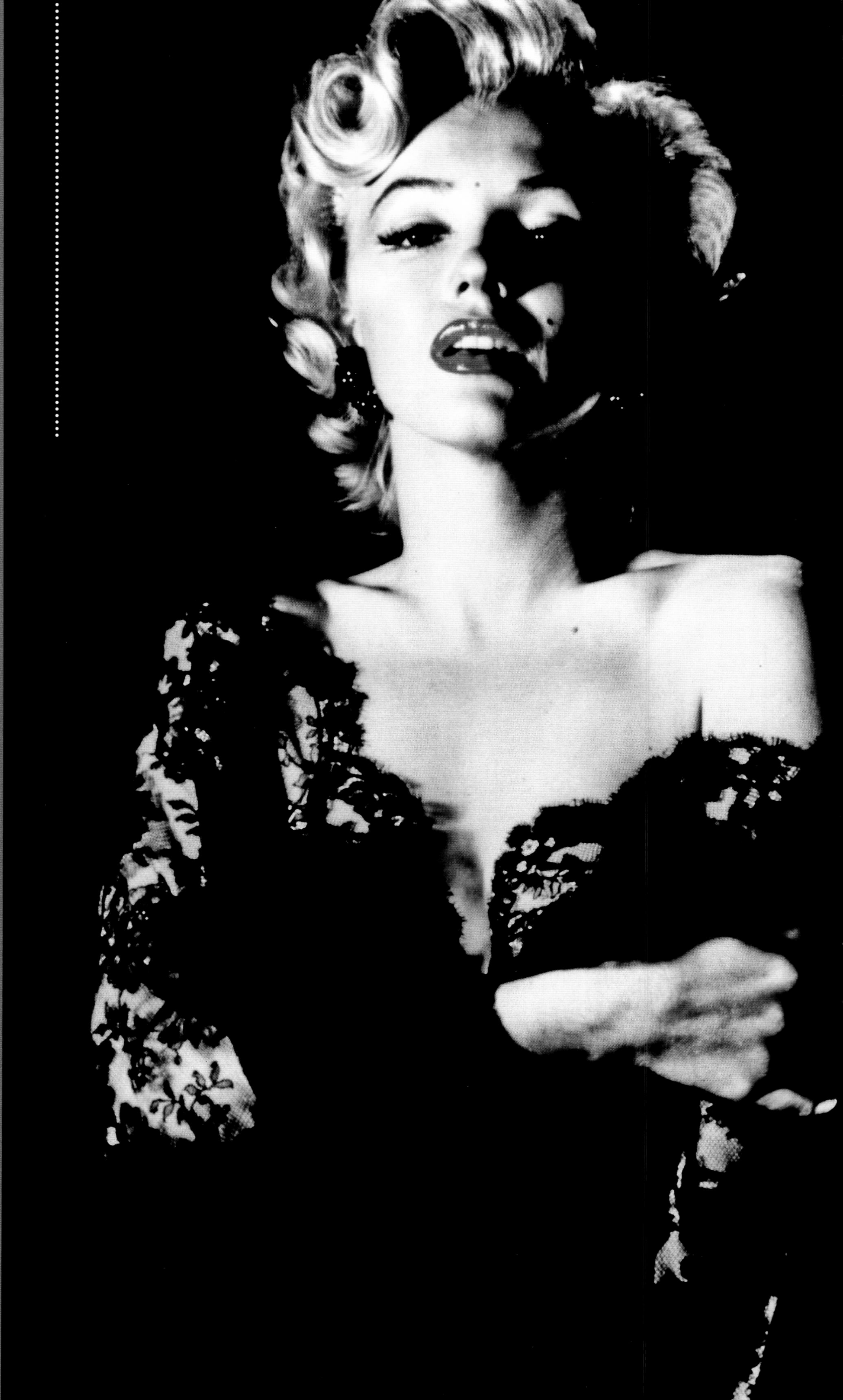

I AM
the blonde

"BEING A SEX SYMBOL IS A HEAVY LOAD TO CARRY, ESPECIALLY
WHEN ONE IS TIRED, HURT, AND BEWILDERED."

For Marilyn's twenty-sixth birthday on June 1, 1952, Fox told her that she would star as Lorelei Lee in the film version of the play *Gentlemen Prefer Blondes*. They had chosen her over Betty Grable, for whom the role was originally planned. Marilyn was ecstatic. And scared.

"The more important she got, the more nervous she got," says Paul Wurtzel, who worked for Fox at the time. Even though she was often in the building on time, she would spend hours in the dressing room getting her makeup done and redone (washing her face and making her makeup artist start over when she wasn't pleased) while she talked herself into walking out onto the set.

The director and crew would whisper and complain about Marilyn's lateness. Marilyn's makeup man told Jane Russell's makeup man that Marilyn was terrified, and that's why she was always late on set. Jane finally asked, "Why doesn't someone just go in there and get her?" And that's just what she did. From then on, Jane would go into Marilyn's dressing room and walk with her onto the set. "Come on, baby, it's almost time. Let's go," she would say.

"Marilyn was very shy and very sensitive. Smart. She really wanted to be very good, and she had a great deal of drive," Jane told *Insight*. She also explained that when the director kicked coach Natasha Lytess off the set one day, Marilyn cried. "She was a very sensitive, sweet little girl."

opposite 1953 PUBLICITY PHOTO, SHOT BY NICKOLAS MURAY.

Perhaps here is where we first see evidence of Marilyn's ability to stand up for herself, though. She knew Fox was getting off cheap. Her contract was structured with specific pay increases, so she'd wind up with only about $18,000 for the film, versus the $150,000 or so they would have had to pay Betty Grable for the same role. She couldn't renegotiate that, but she at least wanted her own dressing room.

As she recalled in her last interview with Richard Meryman of *Life*, she told executives, "'Look, after all, I am the blonde, and it is *Gentlemen Prefer Blondes*!' Because still they always kept saying, 'Remember, you're not a star.' I said, 'Well, whatever I am, I am the blonde!'" She got the dressing room.

She also got to sing a song that became her trademark, although it was almost taken away from her. Marni Nixon, the best-known "voice double" at that time, dubbed the singing parts for such stars as Audrey Hepburn, Natalie Wood, and Deborah Kerr in their famous musicals. Fox taped Marni singing exactly one half of one line for one of Marilyn's song: "These rocks don't lose their shape" in

"Diamonds Are a Girl's Best Friend. " Marni had originally been told that the studio wanted Marilyn's entire singing part dubbed. "Studio head Darryl Zanuck or someone else high up thought her voice was silly. Can you imagine?" Marni wrote in her memoir, *I Could Have Sung All Night*. "Thank goodness they let her sing her own way. That breathless, sexy sound suited her screen persona perfectly, even if she did need a little help on the high notes."

When Marilyn was a young girl dreaming about becoming a star, she would often try matching her hands and feet to the movie stars' prints on the forecourt of Grauman's Chinese Theatre. "I never could get my feet in there—my feet were always too big," she said.

But on June 26, 1953, following the release of *Gentlemen Prefer Blondes*, both she and Jane Russell were invited to put their prints in the cement. Marilyn suggested that, to best represent their fame, Jane should lean forward and leave breast-prints, and she should simply sit in the cement and leave butt-prints! Failing that, she asked for a diamond to dot the "i" in Marilyn, representing her song "Diamonds Are a Girl's Best Friend." It was a wise decision to disallow this; a rhinestone was used instead, but it was soon pried out and stolen.

"This is for all time, isn't it?" Marilyn asked Jane excitedly, as they left their prints. She was overcome with emotion.

Photographer Sam Shaw sometimes brought his son, Larry, along with him on photo shoots as an apprentice. When Larry first met Marilyn, he was a teenager and hadn't thought she was very attractive. "She was a friend of my mother's," he explained. "A guy at seventeen doesn't think much of his mother's friends." Accompanying his father to Marilyn's apartment a few days later, Larry peeked around in the hopes that he might meet Joe DiMaggio, not just the blonde who answered the door in a bathrobe with a glass of champagne in hand.

above IN COSTUME WITH JANE RUSSELL, DURING A BREAK FROM SHOOTING *GENTLEMEN PREFER BLONDES*, 1953. opposite MARILYN AND JANE LEAVE THEIR HAND- AND FOOTPRINTS AT GRAUMAN'S CHINESE THEATRE, 1953.

Larry wasn't particularly interested in photographing Marilyn, but once he did, his perspective changed: "When I looked in the camera at her face, it was transformed . . . different. It was a shock to me . . . because she didn't look like that when you looked at her. She looked like that through the lens."

Over the years, Marilyn became a good friend of the Shaws, and she sometimes took Larry's young sisters out to the circus or museums. "I have to tell you, she kind of annoyed me because she called me 'Kid' all the time. She knew that annoyed me—I guess that's why she kept doing it."

But he was less annoyed when he and his father were walking down 57th Street and ran into Marilyn coming out of a hotel near Central Park. It was a hot summer day, and she was wearing a fur coat.

"How come you're wearing that?" Sam asked.

"Joe just gave it to me. You like?" she asked.

Then she gave an impish smile and flashed them, right on the busy New York street at about two in the afternoon; she wasn't wearing any clothing underneath. They couldn't stop laughing.

"*Then* I thought she was attractive!" Larry said.

Bennett Cerf, founder of Random House, was dying to interview Marilyn, so he wrangled an assignment from *Esquire* magazine. On the day of their scheduled lunch, however, Marilyn called to say she had a cold. If he didn't mind catching it, though, he could come to her hotel room—which he did, finding her in bed in a little nightgown and jacket. On the bed next to her was a thick book.

In his interview for the Oral History Research Office Collection of the Columbia University Libraries, Bennett recalls, "I said, 'You don't have to dress the room up to please me, Marilyn [. . . .] That Modern Library book that you've got there—that's just to impress me, isn't it?' She responded, 'No. Why should it impress you?' She didn't know that I published the Modern Library."

Marilyn went on, "Somebody told me that every educated girl should know about the Essays of Montaigne," and Bennett replied, "You gullible girl! I don't think that anybody outside of college students who have to read the Essays of Montaigne are aware the book is still in print. If you want to read some good Modern Library books, I'll send you a dozen that you'll love."

"Do you seriously mean that I don't have to read this?" Marilyn asked.

Bennet remembers, "With this, to my intense delight, she climbed out of bed, in that little blue bed jacket and a very short nightgown, took the Essays of Montaigne in the tips of her fingers, walked across the room, threw it in the wastebasket—and got back into bed."

Marilyn gathered up all sorts of awards and honors in 1952 and 1953, including *Look* magazine's "Most Promising Female Newcomer" and *Redbook* magazine's "Best Young Box Office Personality." Her appearance at the *Photoplay* awards to receive her "Fastest Rising Star of 1952" plaque, however, caused much uproar.

opposite AT THE FOREIGN PRESS AWARDS IN LOS ANGELES, 1952. above HOLDING HER AWARD FOR "BEST YOUNG BOX OFFICE PERSONALITY."

The dress was the culprit. Low-cut, gold, and so tight that she had to be sewn into it, it was risqué enough that the audience responded with whistles and catcalls.

Joan Crawford made outraged comments about the distastefulness of the dress, and told columnist Bob Thomas, "Certainly her picture isn't doing business, and I'll tell you why. Sex plays a tremendously important part in every person's life. People are interested in it, intrigued with it. But they don't like to see it flaunted in their faces. . . . The publicity has gone too far, and apparently Miss Monroe is making the mistake of believing her publicity. . . . She should be told that the public likes provocative feminine personalities; but it also likes to know that underneath it all, the actresses are ladies."

Marilyn's fans wrote to gossip columnists in outrage. Who was Joan to speak for "the public" about what was appropriate for Marilyn to wear?

Joan's biting remarks weren't completely out of the blue,

however, as she had a bit of history with Marilyn. At one point, Marilyn recalled that Joan told her to make a list of everything in her wardrobe, and Joan would tell her what to buy to go with it to improve her appearance. Marilyn never made that list—partly because she didn't have much of a wardrobe, and partly because she didn't much care what women thought of her clothing choices. Joan wasn't the first or last woman to criticize her for dressing too suggestively. "You would think all other women kept their bodies in vaults," Marilyn said.

"I'm forced to admit that all of my adult life, I've preferred to dress for men rather than for other women," she said in *Modern Screen*. "For this reason, I suppose, I cannot expect other women to appreciate or even to like my clothes. But I do, and I was hurt by the accusation that I have no taste in my manner of dress. It is simply that, during the relatively few years I have been able to afford pretty clothes, I have always been most at ease when I am presenting myself on an unmistakably feminine level. Every suit, every dress, and every gown I own was carefully selected for its potential effect. Personally, too, I feel that if more women followed this same principle, they would be more feminine."

Despite her confident stance about her dress, she was still shaken by Joan's comments.

"I cried all night," Marilyn told gossip columnist Louella Parsons. "I've always admired Miss Crawford for being such a wonderful mother—for taking four children and giving them a fine home. Who better than I knows what that means to homeless little ones?" However, there was one side benefit to the insult: Marilyn got to see how many people wrote to the newspapers to stick up for her, "I'm beginning to look at it as a blessing in disguise. If it had never been printed, I might never have realized how many friends I have, even ones I've never met."

Hoping to end the publicity, Joan said she thought she was talking off the record when she made those comments, and regretted speaking so openly.

above AT THE 1952 *PHOTOPLAY* AWARDS WEARING THE NOTORIOUS DRESS.

SHOWING OFF HER "FASTEST RISING STAR OF
1952" PLAQUE, *PHOTOPLAY* AWARDS NIGHT, 1952.

Marilyn had always been proud of showing off her figure, including her run as the most popular cheesecake model ever. Many stars before Marilyn posed for cheesecake photos only until they had become famous enough to safely thumb their noses at the exploitation. But Marilyn didn't feel exploited; she not only understood that this is where she had truly gotten her start, but she genuinely still enjoyed seducing the still camera, and the attention from men she got as a result.

"I see nothing wrong in cheesecake—if it's honest and in good taste," she told a *Movieland* reporter. "Sex has nothing to do with what you wear or don't wear, with the shape of one's ankle or bosom—but with feeling. There may be more sex appeal in the way you walk and carry yourself or in the flutter of an eyelid than in any amount of clothes-shedding. Not that the right measurements don't help. But after all,

what's wrong with sex appeal? Doesn't every woman want to have it and develop what she has got? I believe in being a well-rounded, complete person as a woman, as a human being. Sex is part of life, it's a part of nature—and I'd rather go along with nature."

Marilyn's sex appeal certainly wasn't ruled by her measurements or her weight, which fluctuated from average to slightly overweight throughout her life. Exercise and diet hadn't been much on her mind before this time ("My single biggest concern used to be getting enough to eat. Now I have to worry about eating too much," she said), but now she began taking walks every morning and working out with light weights for a few minutes every day. She made up her own routine to firm her bust. "I don't count rhythmically like the exercise people on the radio. I couldn't stand exercise if I had to feel regimented about it."

above ONE OF MARILYN'S CHEESECAKE PHOTOS FROM 1953.

The writing was on the wall that Betty Grable was on her way out as Marilyn was on her way in, which must have made people nervous that the two were about to work together in *How to Marry a Millionaire*. But Marilyn stole the show as the nearsighted Pola Debevoise, and Betty couldn't have been kinder to her.

In her autobiography *By Myself and Then Some*, Lauren Bacall, who played Schatze Page, tells what it was like to work with the frightened, insecure Marilyn: "During our scenes she'd look at my forehead instead of my eyes; at the end of a take, look to her coach, standing behind [director] Jean Negulesco, for approval. . . . A scene often went to fifteen or more takes, which meant I had to be good in all of them as no one knew which one would be used. Not easy—often irritating. And yet I couldn't dislike Marilyn. She had no meanness in her—no bitchery. She just had to concentrate on herself and the people who were there only for her."

Marilyn often came across as flighty, losing her focus in a scene. "Very often, the director had to break up a long take as she could not sustain a long delivery," says film editor Orven Schanzer. Dance numbers were difficult for her, and he explains that at times, a "decoy" dancer would do the routine out of range of camera, so she could follow the dancer in front of her.

Lauren felt that there was something innately sad about Marilyn, about her inability to connect with people. Both Lauren and Betty made efforts to help Marilyn feel that she could trust them, though Marilyn rarely spoke with them off the set. Lauren recalled one conversation: "She came into my dressing room one day and said that what she really wanted was to be in San Francisco with Joe DiMaggio in some spaghetti joint. They were not married then. She wanted to know about my children, my home life—was I happy? She seemed envious of that aspect of my life—wistful—hoping to have it herself one day."

Whatever demons might have chased Marilyn, there's no denying she was likable despite them. "Marilyn exuded

a magical charm, and regardless of the problems she created, I never once heard anything derogatory about her," says Orven. "I think this is because Marilyn's relationships with everyone on the set, from grip on up, were genuine and loving ones."

Things weren't quite so pleasant on her next film, *River of No Return*, which Marilyn herself called "a grade-Z cowboy movie where the acting finished third to the scenery and Cinemascope." Marilyn was excited to work with Robert Mitchum, who, before he became an actor, had coincidentally worked with her first husband, James Dougherty, at the Lockheed Plant. She was less excited, however, to work with director Otto Preminger.

Assistant director Paul Helmick told Robert Mitchum's biographer Lee Server, "Otto was a complete pain in the ass. Vicious, impatient, very crude to people, especially to women." In practically no time at all, the director and

above LEFT TO RIGHT: BETTY GRABLE, LAUREN BACALL, AND MARILYN MONROE IN A PUBLICITY STILL FOR *HOW TO MARRY A MILLIONAIRE*, 1953.

WITH A CREW MEMBER ON THE
SET OF *RIVER OF NO RETURN*, 1954.

Marilyn weren't speaking to each other. "Not a word. It was the biggest mismatch I've ever seen. They absolutely detested each other."

What made it worse was Natasha Lytess; the director (and most other people on set) couldn't stand the woman. He hated the way she coached Marilyn to overenunciate her words, but moreover, he just hated her personality. Once, she drove the child playing Robert's son to tears when she told him that child actors lose their talent around his age. That was the last straw for Otto: He threw her off the set.

It didn't last, though. Marilyn made a phone call, and soon, Darryl Zanuck ordered Otto to bring Natasha back. After all, Marilyn was "money in the bank," and the coach promised not to speak to anyone else on the set besides Marilyn anymore.

Marilyn twisted her ankle while filming a scene, and made a big enough deal of it that her leg was put in a cast and Joe DiMaggio came out to take care of her—but Shelley Winters, who also came to visit, said that Marilyn actually had to be reminded that she was supposed to be injured while they were out dancing. The real reason she acted so hurt, Shelley said, was to get some sympathy from the director.

Despite the behind-the-scenes antics, *The New York Times* review sounded very positive for Marilyn: "The mountainous scenery is spectacular, but so, in her own way, is Miss Monroe." But on closer inspection, all the reviewer was complimenting were her beautiful body and clingy costumes. He never mentioned her acting.

After finishing the grueling process of *River of No Return*, Marilyn decided to try to negotiate new terms with the studio. Most importantly, she wanted control over what films she would do, as well as better pay. They announced that she would star in *The Girl in Pink Tights* with Frank Sinatra, but she didn't want to agree to it until she read the script—and she wanted a paycheck that more closely resembled Frank's ($5,000 a week, versus her $1,500). But Darryl Zanuck's message was clear: She could do the film or get her contract suspended.

She didn't do the film. And she did get suspended.

When the day came to begin shooting, she simply didn't show up. Instead, she left for San Francisco to spend time with Joe DiMaggio's family. Possibly just to scare her into coming back, Fox announced that blond dancer Sheree North would become Marilyn's replacement. Marilyn had other things on her mind: On January 14, 1954, she put on an uncharacteristically conservative brown suit with an ermine collar buttoned practically to her chin (Joe didn't like her to look flashy) with a corsage of three white orchids, and went off to marry Joe at the San Francisco city hall. Just before tying the knot, she called Fox publicist Harry Brand to let him know what was happening, and he shot the word out far and wide—more than five hundred people were waiting at city hall when they arrived.

Before the wedding ceremony, the couple answered reporters' questions:

Are you excited, Marilyn? "Oh, you *know* it's more than that!" she said with a giggle.

Where are you going on your honeymoon? "Just driving," said Joe.

How many children are you going to have? "We'll have at least one, I'll guarantee that," Joe said, while Marilyn responded, "I'd like to have six."

The ceremony lasted from 1:46 to 1:48 p.m. A couple of days later, noticing the tremendously positive press for Marilyn, Fox lifted her suspension, asking that she return to work on January 20. She didn't. How about January 25? No?

In the end, she got what she wanted: She would not do *The Girl in the Pink Tights*, and she'd get a raise and a vacation: She was off to Japan for her honeymoon.

left JOE DIMAGGIO KISSES HIS NEW BRIDE
FOLLOWING THE CEREMONY IN SAN FRAN-
CISCO. opposite MR. AND MRS. JOE DIMAGGIO
PRESS THROUGH A CROWD OF NEWSMEN
AFTER THEIR MARRIAGE IN THE OFFICE OF
MUNICIPAL JUDGE CHARLES PEERY.

CHAPTER SEVEN

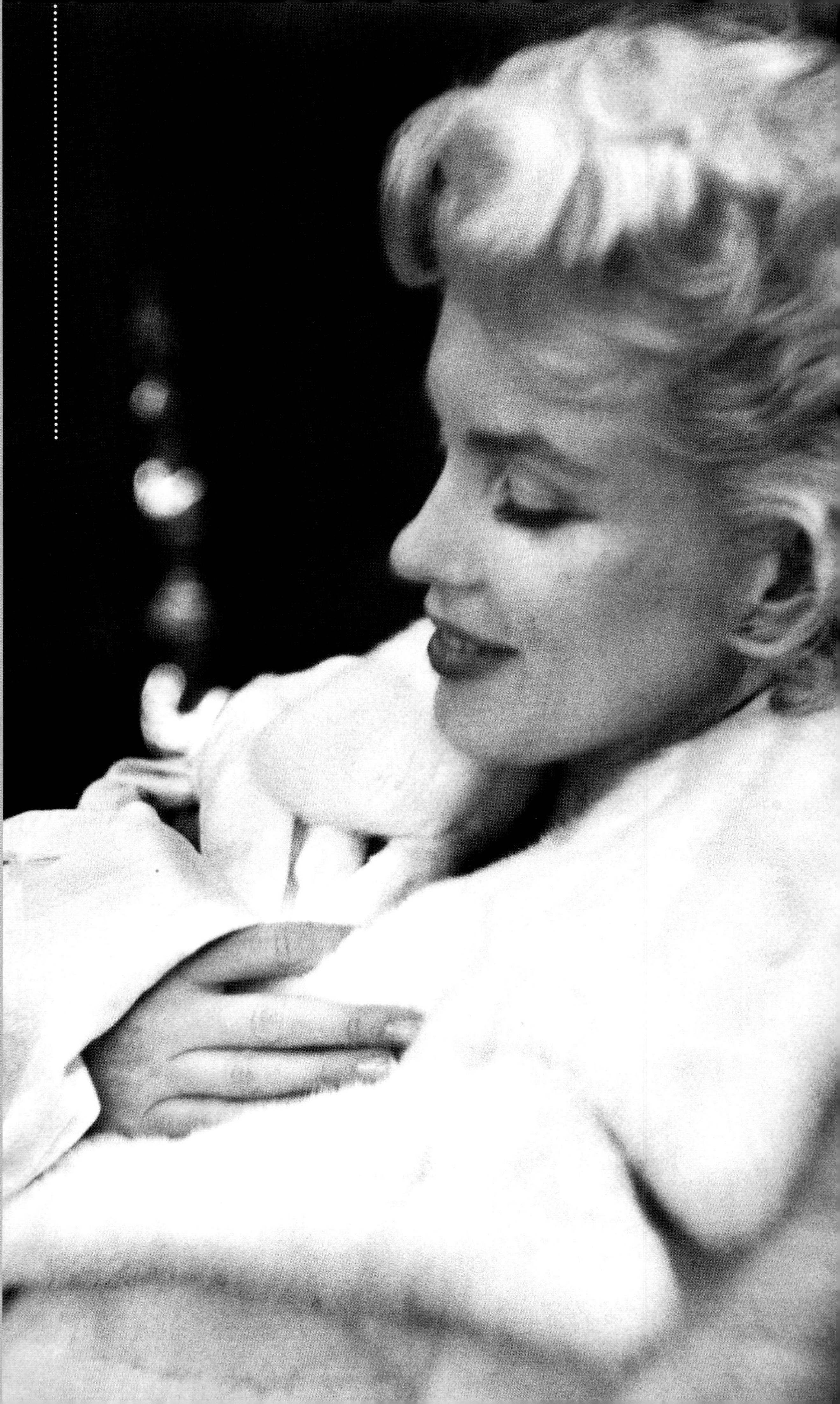

COCOONING

"FIRST, I'M TRYING TO PROVE TO MYSELF THAT I'M A PERSON. THEN MAYBE I'LL CONVINCE MYSELF THAT I'M AN ACTRESS."

Joe and Marilyn's wedding was a spur-of-the-moment decision, so it wasn't particularly odd that the honeymoon was part of a business trip Joe had already planned—he was going with his best man and former baseball manager "Lefty" O'Doul as a coach on a goodwill tour. Lefty simply called in an extra plane ticket for Marilyn, and they were off to Tokyo. While they were there, a U.S. Army officer suggested that it would be a great morale booster for the troops in Korea if Marilyn came to entertain. She agreed, despite Joe's objections.

For a week, she rehearsed with the servicemen who played in the "Anything Goes" band in Osaka, where band leader Don Obermeyer discovered that she was much different from what he would have expected from a Hollywood star. "She was very easy to get along with. Just charming," he says. "Until we rehearsed in Osaka, she had never seen an upright microphone before—everything [in Hollywood] was booms overhead—and she walked up to it like she was afraid of it, but she soon learned to use it. She did just about everything we asked her to do. She was so willing to be cooperative and nice. I don't think she had a mean bone in her body."

She rehearsed over and over, continually asking what the band needed and how she could do better. After rehearsals, they flew to Busan. Don says, "She was in the front of the airplane with all the colonels and majors . . . and she excused herself and came back and sat down with each and every one of us in the soldier group and wanted to know where we're from, where

opposite WEARING WHITE FUR IN NEW YORK, 1955.

we went to school, what our ambitions were, how big our families were, our hometowns, interesting little tidbits . . . she wanted to know more about us. She didn't want to be with the brass, she wanted to be with 'the guys.' "

The "Anything Goes" band spent the next week together traveling around Korea, doing twenty-three shows. Although she wasn't accustomed to performing live, she decided to sing several songs for the troops, including her trademark "Diamonds Are a Girl's Best Friend," which she wasn't sure about initially—she thought it might be inconsiderate to sing about diamonds when the soldiers didn't make enough money to buy them, but then decided that the dance she did at the end of the number would make up for it.

It was snowing when the first show began, and she was wearing a spaghetti-strapped cocktail dress.

"The highlight of my life was singing for the soldiers there," she said later. "I stood out on an open stage. I was cold, but I swear I didn't feel a thing except good."

John T. Jones was a soldier who saw her perform, and says, "Marilyn knocked herself out for the troops. While planes were strafing just north of us, she sang, joked, and gave the troops a good show. They were appreciative and gave her much applause. After the show, some of my guys went up by the stage and got her autograph and photos. I knew Marilyn because she was on the radio at night on the Armed Forces Radio Network. Yes, we loved that gal—hated to see her get kicked around in life."

Ed Barrus remembers going down the dusty roads to see "the one and only." "When we arrived at our destination, we tried to spruce up in case she called out to one of us to come up on stage with her . . . we were a bunch of dreamers. They had some other entertainers perform—they did a good job, but we wanted to see Marilyn. Finally, she came up to the stage in a tank. I do not blame her; that was the safest way. Well, she backed out of the tank and we saw her backside. Now the G.I.s were screaming. We did not care whether she could sing or not, we just stood there and stared at her. She

above A CROWD OF U.S. SOLDIERS GREET MARILYN AS SHE STEPS OFF THE PLANE IN KOREA, 1954. opposite (top) WAVING TO THE TROOPS. opposite (bottom) ACCOMPANIED ON BASE BY AN ARMY ESCORT.

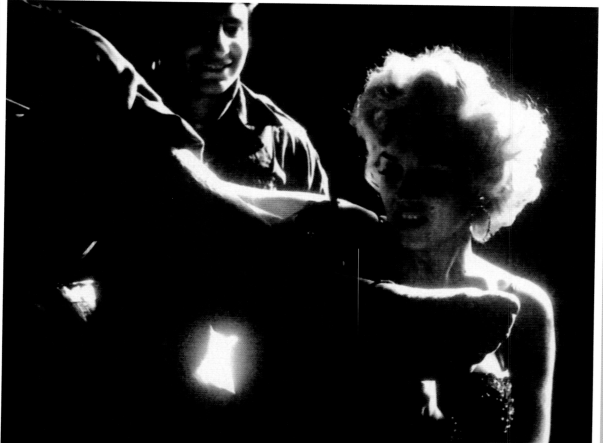

was very beautiful. I felt my three-year enlistment was worth it, even though I was about forty rows back."

Marilyn enjoyed herself just as much. "For the first time in my life, I felt I belonged, that people saw me and accepted me, liked me . . . for the first time, I felt like a movie star," she said.

At each stop they made on the tour, Marilyn was invited to the officers' club to receive V.I.P. treatment. The first time someone tried to usher her off, she gestured to the band and said, "I'm not going to that officers' club without my guys. Where I go, they go." That's the way it was all across Korea, Don says. "She insisted that [the band] be with her, so we were in some nice officers' clubs!"

By the end of the trip in February 1954, she had a fever and pneumonia, but she was still joyful. When she reunited with Joe in Japan, she was flushed with excite-

ment, telling him, "You never heard such cheering!" He responded, "Yes, I have."

There were some obvious problems in Joe and Marilyn's marriage right away, and some concern among friends that there might have been violence between them. Marilyn had an array of bruises with an odd explanation—"I bite myself in my sleep," she told people on the set of *There's No Business Like Show Business*. But there was also love between them.

Joe kept this note, scribbled on the back of a dry cleaning receipt, in a wallet until he died: "Dear Joe, I know I was wrong! I acted the way I did and said the things I did because I was hurt—not because I meant them—and it was stupid of me to be hurt because actually there wasn't enough reason—in fact no reason at all. Please accept my

opposite (top) POSING WITH DON OBERMEYER (TOP LEFT) AND OTHER SOLDIERS IN KOREA. opposite (bottom) AUTO-GRAPHING A SOLDER'S LEG. above PERFORMING FOR AN ATTENTIVE AUDIENCE IN FEBRUARY 1954.

apology and don't, don't, don't, don't be angry with your baby—she loves you. Lovingly, your wife (for life), Mrs. J. P. DiMaggio."

Nevertheless, Joe's distaste for Marilyn's career only grew. He rarely showed up on her set, and when he did, he wasn't happy; he saw Hollywood as a bunch of phonies and hated the sort of roles the studios assigned to Marilyn. Within a couple of months, she moved out of Joe's house and began an affair with her vocal coach, Hal Schaefer.

Hal and Marilyn had worked together twice before, on *Gentlemen Prefer Blondes* and *River of No Return*. He liked Marilyn from the start and felt that she was unlike most movie stars. She didn't have a big ego or a false persona— he realized that she was very sweet and a bit shy, with little self-esteem. Looking at her, he said, you always felt like she had been through a lot of hurt.

It wasn't until they met again on the set of *There's No Business Like Show Business* in May 1954 that a romantic relationship developed. "It just happened," he says. "We fell in love with each other."

Morally, he says, he would never have gotten involved with a married woman, but he didn't consider Marilyn married. She was not legally divorced, but she had told him that she left Joe and had no plans of ever reuniting. He had also seen bruises on her face and heard the silly excuses, like "I walked into a door."

"Would you just play?" she would ask him some nights, sitting on the floor in her apartment, with him at her white piano. "I love the way you play. I love your touch, the sound . . . it gives me such a feeling, like great medicine." Then she would just listen, off in a reverie.

Hal ardently claims that Marilyn wasn't always a drinker or pill-popper. In those days, she was squeaky clean, even when he tried to talk her into having a drink with him. "I would say, 'Come on, Sweetheart, have a drink.' She'd say, 'I don't like it very much. I don't like the way it tastes.

I feel good, this is nice, and I like being with you. I don't need that.'"

He would sneak her to his parents' apartment, where his mother would cook Jewish food—meatballs and latkes. Marilyn was in heaven, he says, so he started taking her to Canter's, a famous deli on Fairfax Avenue in Los Angeles's Jewish section.

"She had a great costume, and we thought we were fooling everybody. She had a ratty black wig; she wore oversized dark glasses; she wore a dress that was big enough for a 250-pound lady, old shoes. . . . She'd look like she was in disguise . . . and nobody recognized her. How could they?"

Hal says they were going to get married as soon as her divorce was final, and she was planning to convert to Judaism for him. Meanwhile, though, rumors about their romance were starting to spread.

Hal's good friend at Fox, Lionel Newman, took him aside one day and said, "Nix it with Marilyn." At first, Hal

opposite ON THE SET OF *THERE'S NO BUSINESS LIKE SHOW BUSINESS*, 1954. above HAL SCHAEFER WITH MARILYN ON THE SET OF *RIVER OF NO RETURN*, 1954.

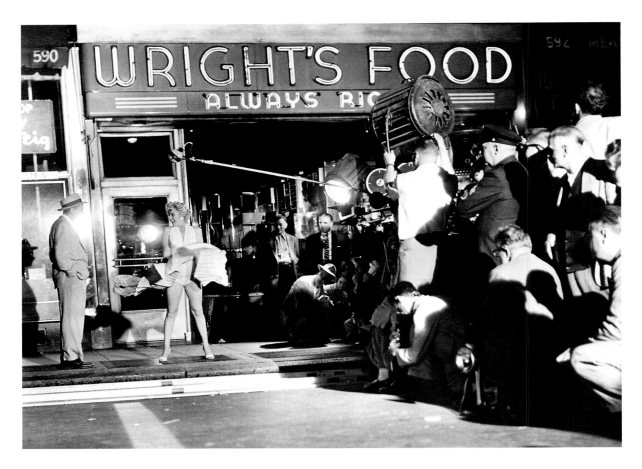

pretended not to know what he was talking about, but he could see that wasn't going to work.

He thought back to a day when he and Marilyn both had breaks at the same time, so they met on the "curb" of a phony street that was part of a set on the lot. It must have turned heads, seeing Marilyn with this pianist . . . who was he to be talking to her? He wasn't her costar or a famous actor. And sometimes, he says, you can't help it—two people in love tend to look at each other like they're in love.

So maybe that's all it took. "She told me she likes me and I like her," Hal confessed to Lionel. "We dig each other. Is there a law against it?"

"I'm telling you this is going to be nothing but big-time trouble," Lionel said. But obviously, Hal didn't listen.

Right after *There's No Business Like Show Business*, Marilyn began work on *The Seven Year Itch*. One of the most famous images in history was made on this film: Marilyn's "skirt blowing" scene above a subway grate. At 52nd Street and Lexington Avenue, special effects man Paul Wurtzel stood in the subway station below with a giant fan, and Marilyn stood above wearing two pairs of underwear—because just one was too see-through—letting the fan blow her skirt up.

The scene attracted literally thousands of onlookers, both media professionals and the general public, and they worked themselves into a frenzy, calling out, "Higher! Higher!" Joe DiMaggio's friend Walter Winchell, a top gossip columnist, convinced him to go watch Marilyn's shoot that night. Did Walter orchestrate this because he knew Joe was going to react badly to what was going on that night and provide great fodder for his gossip column? If so, he got what he wanted. In the midst of the scene, Joe walked over and was horrified. There was Marilyn, putting on what appeared to be a burlesque show for all of New York City.

"What the hell's going on here?" he asked before storming off.

above THE CREW OF *THE SEVEN YEAR ITCH* GATHERS AROUND MARILYN TO FILM THE INFAMOUS SUBWAY GRATE SCENE IN MANHATTAN, OCTOBER 1954.

CO-STAR TOM EWELL LOOKS ON AS MARILYN
MANAGES HER WIND-BLOWN DRESS.

They had an explosive fight that night that may have become violent. The marriage was over. She officially separated from him three weeks later, on October 4, 1954, and the first divorce hearing was held on October 27. Although she didn't fully explain to the press what went wrong in their marriage, she gave a few coy hints, such as "I think TV sets should be taken out of the bedroom."

Despite his anger, Joe was devastated, and couldn't bear the thought of Marilyn with another man. She refused to speak with him and had been avoiding him since they separated, which he moaned about to Frank Sinatra. Joe had desperately been trying to track her down, and even hired detectives to look for her, to no avail. So, as a favor to Joe, Frank hired his own private investigator to find her.

While Joe, Frank, and several others were at a bar on November 5, they got word that she had been found in an apartment, presumably with Hal. After a quick sidetrip to another bar to get burly actor Brod Crawford, who they figured would be capable of breaking the door down if needed, the group set out to the apartment building, causing a drunken ruckus once they got there.

Marilyn and Hal were indeed there, upstairs in the building. The apartment belonged to one of Hal's former students who had become a friend of his. He had complained to her one day, "I have such a problem because I have this thing with Marilyn and she has a thing with me and we can't meet anyplace and spend any time alone." The woman told him she was going out of town on a particular weekend, and gave him the key to her apartment. "I'm your friend. Mum's the word if you want to take Marilyn there. There won't be anyone there."

So Marilyn and Hal had each parked a couple of blocks away from the apartment and met up there. They had no clue that their cars were bugged and that they were both being followed by detectives. They were half-undressed in bed when they heard something unsettling out front.

"I opened the blinds a little bit and saw all these goons across the street with Sinatra and DiMaggio standing right there. It was terrifying. It was absolutely terrifying. Poor Marilyn was going to come apart. 'What can we do? What can we do?' There were eight or ten of them, and they looked like goons. One was a private detective who had been a cop with the Beverly Hills Police Department."

Because of the odd construction of the building, though, the front door that appeared to lead to the upstairs apartment actually led to the main-floor apartment. The entrance for the upstairs apartment was around the side of the building. So the men, carrying flashlights, barreled down the wrong door around 11 p.m.—and a fifty-year-old woman, Florence Kotz Ross, awoke in her bed and screamed in fright, apparently suffering a mild heart attack in the process.

It was a miracle for Marilyn and Hal, who managed to flee and run to their cars during the commotion. Hal was sure that if those men had found them, he would have been permanently injured, at the very least. Florence recognized

opposite (top and bottom) OCTOBER 6, 1954, MARILYN LEAVES THE HOME SHE SHARED WITH DIMAGGIO. above PICTURE TAKEN THROUGH THE CAR WINDOW AS MARILYN IS DRIVEN AWAY.

Frank Sinatra, and initiated a lawsuit against her famous intruders, eventually settling for $7,500.

Just three days after the raid, Marilyn had gynecological surgery. She had frequent gynecological problems and treatments through her life for endometriosis, which caused her significant pain. Joe, ever faithful despite the circumstances, stayed with her in the hospital for hours.

Hal was petrified that these men would track him down and kill him and was brokenhearted that he couldn't be with Marilyn in peace. "I couldn't find a solution," he said. "The only solution was to get out of this whole thing, to be done with this world. I don't know how many sleeping pills I took, but the main thing was I drank two kinds of liquid poison: One was like turpentine, the other was typewriter cleaning fluid. There must've been a bottle somewhere in my office in my supplies, and I drank it. I can still remem-

ber it had a really bitter taste, like wine gone sour. It was not a little attention-getter, because it took me a whole year to recuperate."

There were two doctors on Hal's case, and one of them said, "This man is dead" and walked off. Actually, he was in a coma, and a fast-thinking male nurse suggested that they try injecting Hal with as much caffeine as they could; it worked enough for them to resuscitate him. Marilyn sneaked in to visit him at the hospital, but he was too out of it to remember anything about the visit.

Upon his release, Hal left Los Angeles and went up the California coast to a secret home by the ocean to recuperate for several months, hiring the male nurse to stay with him. Marilyn came to visit him there a couple of times, and once asked if they could be intimate.

Hal recalls, "She wanted to know if I felt well enough, or if it would help me with my recuperation, or whatever. She

above FRANK SINATRA (FAR LEFT) BEING SWORN IN AT THE INVESTIGATION OF THE "WRONG DOOR RAID."

really was a very feeling soul, a lovely human being. Beautiful inside as she was outside, even though it's an old cliché."

The trip would take her several hours because she'd continually drive out of the way on long, winding paths to make sure she wasn't being followed, and she'd stop to check the car for any signs of bugging devices. Although she never found any, the last time she came to visit, the nurse looked out the window and saw an unfamiliar car parked half a block down. He didn't like the looks of it, so he told Marilyn he thought she should leave. That day in Hal's room in 1955 was the last time the couple would see each other.

About a year earlier, a young photographer, Milton Greene, had photographed Marilyn for *Look* magazine's holiday issue. The two hit it off instantly and met up again at a party a few days later. He was just about to get married and have a baby, and his interest in Marilyn wasn't romantic, but he saw something wonderfully special about her.

"This woman was a chameleon in front of the camera," says Milton's son, Joshua Greene. He saw that, as a model, she could create any mood, conveying a huge range of emotions. Joshua says, "[My father] transposed that into believing that, with practice and the right teaching and mentors, she could do it with her acting—which is what she wanted, but Fox wouldn't give her that ability. They never treated her with that kind of respect."

Milton had no film experience, but it had always been an interest of his. He offered to have his lawyers look over Marilyn's contract with Fox to see if it could be broken. The lawyers found multiple flaws and loopholes that allowed Milton to move to the next step of his plan, which was to set up a production company of their own (Marilyn Monroe Productions), where she could choose what kinds of projects to do and get a much bigger share of the profits.

"I feel wonderful. I'm incorporated!" she said at a press conference. She explained that she was tired of playing the dumb blonde parts and would like to tackle more challenging

roles, like Grushenka in *The Brothers Karamazov* by Dostoevsky. The media made a joke of her ambitions, which troubled her deeply.

"If I say I want to grow as an actress, people look at my figure," she later said. "If I say I want to develop, to learn my craft, they laugh. Somehow, they don't expect me to be serious about my work. I'm more serious about that than anything."

Milton wanted to get Marilyn away from the glitz and glamour of Hollywood and into a place where he felt she could learn a lot more about real acting: New York. That fit right in with her thoughts—she was tired of fighting with the studio about the roles she played. "If you can't do what you want to do, the thing to do is leave," she said. So, only three months after she had announced her divorce from Joe, Marilyn bought a plane ticket under the name "Zelda Zonk" and moved into the Greene household in Weston, Connecticut, traveling into New York City often. Milton also had a small apartment in the city that she used when she wanted to.

Once or twice, Marilyn called Hal, but it was mostly to end things. Hal remembers that he probably said unkind

above PHOTOGRAPHER MILTON GREENE WITH MARILYN.

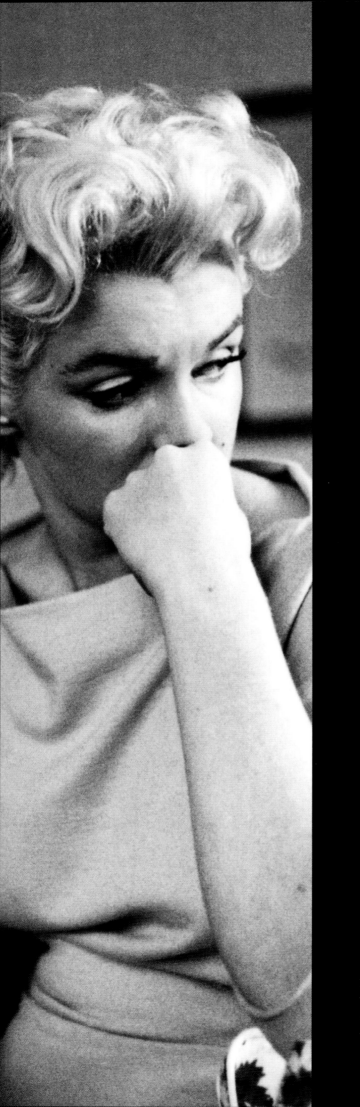

left IN A MANHATTAN HOTEL ROOM, MARCH 1955. opposite OVERLOOKING NEW YORK FROM THE BALCONY OF HER ROOM AT AMBASSADOR HOTEL.

in one picture after another I wore pink tights or yellow tights or green tights."

And by the time the public tired of her, she feared, she would have become accustomed to a life of luxury and have trouble losing it. At this stage, though, she had acquired very little monetarily, so she didn't feel it was as much of a gamble.

"She lived at our house and had the feeling of being in a secure, organized household with a husband and wife who were madly in love with each other and a child who had just been born," says Joshua. "In the fifties, people would get together Saturday nights for charades, and dinner poker nights on Wednesdays were very common. We had huge charades parties—about thirty people split into two teams of fifteen. Lots of different types of people would come over, and she found herself in a different world of artists and writers—a different environment from Hollywood power moguls."

That New Year's Eve, Frank Sinatra was playing at the Copacabana, and Milton's wife, Amy, mentioned over dinner, "Boy, I'd love to go see Frank at the Copa." Marilyn responded, "You want to see Frank? I can arrange it." To Amy's amazement, the moment they arrived, they were escorted past the crowds through the kitchen and over to a VIP table right near the stage, even though the show was already in progress. Frank stopped for a few beats, looked at them, and said, "I just want to make sure Miss Monroe and the Greenes are comfortable before I continue with my performance."

"My mother is somewhat claustrophobic," said Joshua. "She's very petite, and as they were about to leave, everybody crowded Marilyn and Milton and her at the table, and she started feeling claustrophobic. She said, 'I have to get out of here. I'm getting scared,' and Marilyn just parted the Red Sea. She just walked with a sense of 'I'm not talking to anybody now. Stay with me.'"

Amy became a mentor of Marilyn's, too, in a sense; she taught Marilyn how to run a household. It was really

things about Milton in that last call—he believed Milton was brainwashing her to leave him behind. But she said, "Don't blame him. Milton is a friend of mine. It's just that I'm here and we need time . . . if it's supposed to be, it will be."

It took Hal a long time to get over Marilyn, but he eventually moved back to New York and met his soulmate, Brenda, who shared the same birthday as Marilyn.

During 1955, Marilyn was basically in hiding, defusing from her hectic life. When newspaper columnist Elsa Maxwell told Marilyn how brave she was to leave Hollywood, Marilyn countered, "To have stayed took more courage than I had. All any of us has is what we carry with us, the satisfaction we get from what we're doing and the way we're doing it. I had no sense of satisfaction at all. And I was scared. I know that I always tire of anyone who's the same all the time. So I could see how people soon enough would get tired of me—with the only difference in my screen roles being that

above IN THE SUBWAY STATION BENEATH GRAND CENTRAL STATION IN MANHATTAN, MARCH 1955.

Milton who cared deeply about Marilyn, but Amy didn't mind having her as a houseguest. She was a good babysitter, for one thing.

Joshua has happy memories of his childhood years with Marilyn as well: "Being tickled a lot, lots of love, being chased with pillows around the house, bouncing off a wall . . . It was a nice, innocent time."

Marilyn loved children, in part because she didn't question their motives. As time went on, she was growing more and more distrustful of people in general. They all wanted something from her, she figured—they all had an agenda. And certainly, she was right about that much of the time, but sometimes, she pushed people away based on the smallest offense—or on something she interpreted strangely as against her when it was most likely innocuous.

She always seemed to be looking for a "family," though. When she ran into old friend Diana Hubert from *Scudda Hoo! Scudda Hay!*, Diana was pregnant. "I remember her being so wistful. She was grateful to see how happy I was and kept patting my tummy. I knew she would have wanted to have a child, but we didn't go into anything because she

above WITH MILTON AT A HOLLYWOOD PRESS CONFERENCE IN FEBRUARY 1956.

TALKING ON THE PHONE,
ONE OF HER FAVORITE HOBBIES.

wasn't married at the time. But we talked about how having a baby changed your thoughts about career and direction."

Marilyn's mental state was shaky, however. She grew more interested in pills and alcohol as loneliness crept in and as her insomnia worsened.

Since she didn't have a family of her own, Marilyn would latch on to someone else's—Milton Greene's, poet Norman Rosten's, actor Eli Wallach's, or photographer Sam Shaw's. Larry Shaw, Sam Shaw's son, remembers, "Eventually, there were so many phone calls coming into the house from Marilyn that my mother couldn't take it anymore, two and three o'clock in the morning. She had so many problems that you couldn't be in the middle. She was calling because of depression after she had taken pills." He says his parents often had to drive to see her in Manhattan because she had threatened to kill herself or had taken too many pills.

"You know who I always depend on? Not strangers, not friends. The telephone!" Marilyn once said. "That's my best friend. I seldom write letters, but I love calling friends, especially late at night, when I can't sleep."

Marilyn had long wanted to meet Lee Strasberg, an acting teacher and artistic director at the Actors Studio. Lee is considered the father of Method acting, where actors use their emotions and experiences to interpret their characters. Because she was too scared to study with a group at first, Lee gave her free private lessons in his home. He was beyond impressed.

"Despite the bad mannerisms and habits she may have acquired in Hollywood, and with all the abuse she was subjected to, they haven't touched what is underneath," he told his family after dinner, according to his daughter Susan's book *Marilyn and Me*. "It's difficult because you have to look past what she looks like to see what's hidden. She had to hide it or she'd have been too vulnerable to survive, and she's so eager and willing, as if she's a flower that's been waiting all this time for someone to water her."

He told his family that, after Marlon Brando, Marilyn had the greatest raw talent he had ever come across. His encouragement meant everything to Marilyn, who felt that someone was finally taking her seriously, seeing beyond her sex appeal, and believing that she could be a genuine actress.

After three months, she joined the classes at the Actors Studio and was also allowed to observe, a rare privilege.

"Marilyn came to us after she'd achieved a certain standing," Lee said in *American Theatre* magazine. "Everybody said, 'She's going to be spoiled. Why is she coming here? Let her depend on her native talent and naïveté.' But it is clear from the results that she was helped by receiving the proper kind of training. Often in the profession there is a great degree of guilt on the part of people who have made it. Why did the audience single them out? In their own eyes, they haven't achieved what they came into the profession to do, and they are miserable."

above LEE STRASBERG IN LONDON, 1956.

Founding member Kevin McCarthy met Marilyn during her time in New York and remembers that even when he was sitting right next to her at the Actors Studio, he didn't recognize her at first. She looked so different with her hair and makeup undone and plain clothing—just another face in the crowd.

Kevin says she was funny and gracious. "I did a scene one day at the Actors Studio that was quite a success. . . . I was receiving congratulations and comments, and Marilyn suddenly tiptoed over, down the steps and across the floor. She came over and kissed me on the cheek, and whispered, 'It must be wonderful to be you.' She thought I was an actor and she was not. She had trouble with the fact that she wasn't 'it.' She *was* it, of course. She could be a marvelous actress."

On the few days when Marilyn performed scenes, the place was packed—probably equally with people who were there to see her because they were genuinely interested and people who couldn't wait to scoff at the talentless movie star. But she amazed and disarmed her critics. After her first big scene, the place rumbled with applause, a practice normally discouraged at the Actors Studio. Some of the stage actors even came up to her afterward to admit they were wrong about her; she was a real actress, after all.

It meant so much to Marilyn to be accepted by her peers. Despite how well her career was going, she didn't feel she was yet a very good actress, and she didn't feel she had anything else in her life to give it meaning. Her depression ran deep, and little things could set her off screaming or crying.

Lee told her that she needed to be in therapy before he could work with her, but he also partly filled a therapist role for her—and a father role. She stayed at his house, becoming a surrogate daughter who desperately needed coddling. He held her and sang her lullabies when she couldn't sleep, he comforted and counseled her about everything from career to love, and brought her to bed when she'd taken too many pills. Lee's daughter, Susan, remembered being disturbed to see Marilyn crawling through the halls in a stupor.

Although other facets of her creativity are rarely acknowledged, Marilyn's interest in the arts extended beyond film. She wrote poetry that probably would have surprised those who dismissed her as a dumb blonde:

"To the Weeping Willow"
I stood beneath your limbs
And you flowered and finally
clung to me,
and when the wind struck with the earth
and sand—you clung to me.
Thinner than a cobweb I,
sheerer than any—
but it did attach itself
and held fast in strong winds
life—of which at singular times
I am both of your directions—
Somehow I remain hanging downward the most,
As both of your directions pull me.

This highly personal poem seems to allude to her depression ("hanging downward") and her desire for connection (the repetition of "clung to me"). Its imagery is poignantly similar to that in Elton John's "Candle in the Wind" tribute song written by Bernie Taupin long after Marilyn's death: a frail creature in strong winds looking for something to cling to.

Visual art also captured her interest. Larry Shaw once took a trip with his father and Marilyn to see a Goya exhibit at the Museum of Fine Art; Marilyn was enraptured by the pictures, talking like a true artist. "She *was* an artist," he said.

"She always had a fondness for people who are talented, whether in theater or writing or the arts," says Joshua Greene. "She enjoyed being with people who had talent as opposed to money. Money for the sake of money or power for the sake

opposite OUTSIDE THE ACTORS STUDIO IN MANHATTAN, DECEMBER 1956.

of power didn't impress her quite in the same way as people with talent and a gift."

And indeed, she was in awe of those who she saw as being at the top of their fields. Ella Fitzgerald had become her favorite singer, and when she found out that a popular club had refused to book Ella because she was black, Marilyn took action.

According to her official website, Ella said, "I owe Marilyn Monroe a real debt. It was because of her that I played the Mocambo, a very popular nightclub in the '50s. She personally called the owner of the Mocambo, and told him she wanted me booked immediately, and if he would do it, she would take a front table every night. She told him—and it was true, due to Marilyn's superstar status—that the press would go wild. The owner said yes, and Marilyn was there, front table, every night. The press went overboard. After that, I never had to play a small jazz club again. She was an unusual woman—a little ahead of her times. And she didn't know it."

One of Marilyn's quirkiest appearances was in the town of Bement, Illinois, population 1,500, where she was to judge a "Best Beard" contest, visit the town's nursing home and art museum, and give a speech about Abraham Lincoln as part of the town's centennial celebration on August 6, 1955. Carleton Smith, head of the National Arts Foundation, apparently told Marilyn that her presence at the local art exhibit would help "bring art to the masses." It's interesting that she agreed: It wasn't exactly a bustling town of movers and shakers, she didn't need the publicity, and she was still on hiatus in New York at the time. She was an artist at heart, though, and that may have been enough to draw her there.

Her hairdresser accompanied her and Eve Arnold followed to take photographs. Illinois State Police Sergeant Dick "Jiggs" Robison and trooper Dixie Davis were charged with taking Marilyn to and from the airport and protecting her on her visit. It's a good thing, too, because the town was pandemonium, its population nearly quadrupled with people from far and wide gathering to glimpse Marilyn.

"She was having kidney problems at the time, and forgot her medicine," says Dick's daughter, Dicka Wagner. So they went to Carleton Smith's house, where people actually climbed on neighbors' rooftops to try to peek inside. "She had to go in and lie down because her ankles were swelling. Someone broke the door off the house that day."

above WITH ELLA FITZGERALD LISTENING TO JAZZ AT HOLLYWOOD'S TIFFANY CLUB. opposite (above) SIGNING AN AUTOGRAPH IN ILLINOIS. opposite (bottom) WITH DICK ROBISON (LEFT) AND DIXIE DAVIS (RIGHT) AS ESCORTS.

It was raining by the time they drove back to the airport, and Dick drove the speed limit. "Could you step on it, Sergeant?" she asked. "I want to get back to New York!"

He later told his friend Bob Broverman that it was difficult to drive any faster when he spent the whole trip looking at her lovely face in the rearview mirror. But then they realized that planes weren't taking off from the local airport, so the officers decided to drive her all the way to the Chicago airport. First, though, Dick had to let his wife know that he was driving "Miss Monroe" to Chicago. "Quit your damn lyin'!" she'd said.

Marilyn put her bare feet up in the backseat and asked the officers questions about the town, and landmarks she saw out the window. She seemed more interested in talking about them than herself. Although she called Dick "Sergeant," she wouldn't let him call her "Miss Monroe."

"Call me Marilyn," she said. "Sergeant, it's so nice of you to drive us."

When he told her how much of a thrill it was for him to drive her, she said, "Oh no, I'm the one who owes you. I'm just happy to be able to be here, to have you drive me all the way to Chicago." She signed an autograph in his police notebook before leaving.

Dicka says that her father carried around a photograph of Marilyn with them in his squad car for years afterward, whipping it out at the slightest excuse—showing it to waitresses and cashiers all over town, and jokingly charging people a quarter for a tour of the seat where Marilyn sat.

Back at home, Marilyn's fate with the studio was tied to the results of *The Seven Year Itch*. It opened to big box-office dollars and solid reviews, such as *Hollywood Reporter*'s: "Marilyn is just about perfect in the role of the pleasantly vacuous and even more pleasantly curved heroine." After the film proved a success, Fox finally caved in to Marilyn's demands. They needed her. They may have resented her, hated her behavior, underestimated her talent, and wished they could fire her a hundred times over, but she made money for them. People went to movie theaters to see Marilyn Monroe. Despite her dwindling self-esteem, she knew she was a box-office smash and deserved a better contract.

No one had ever made a studio beg for mercy quite like Marilyn did. They gave her director approval and cinematographer approval; she would appear only in "A-films"; and she'd get a large raise—$100,000 per movie. She would also be free to make films with other studios and independently. Of all of it, director approval was the most important to her: "No good director is going to make a bad script or miscast the picture."

She signed her new contract on New Year's Eve of 1955, ending her hiatus. The "new" Marilyn Monroe was ready to go back to show Hollywood what she had learned.

above A SCRAP OF PAPER AUTOGRAPHED BY MARILYN DURING HER ILLINOIS VISIT.

THE "NEW" MARILYN AT A COCKTAIL
PARTY IN MANHATTAN, 1955.

CHAPTER EIGHT

WE'RE
all afraid

"HAVE I GROWN? I DON'T LIKE THE WORD 'GROW.' SOMEHOW,
PEOPLE EXPECT TO SEE ADDED INCHES."

Marilyn's first project under the new contract with Fox was *Bus Stop*, a coproduction with Marilyn Monroe Productions. For the first time, critics really applauded Marilyn's acting skills. She wasn't just hailed as being great eye candy or a funny diversion in *Bus Stop*. People would come to criticize Lee (and his wife, Paula) Strasberg plenty, but it's clear that they brought out something great in Marilyn in her first work since their tutelage.

She underplayed her own beauty by making herself look pale and worn, and rejected the wardrobe originally offered in favor of more tattered clothes. She played a scene nude under the sheets because she decided her character, Cherie, would be nude. But she failed to charm her costar, Don Murray, who she thought wasn't experienced enough to star opposite her. During one scene, she was supposed to lightly smack him with the tail of her costume, but did it so hard that his face was bleeding—then she refused to apologize.

And she decided that Hope Lange's hair was too blond, so she demanded that it be dyed light brown, and walked off the set when the director refused. Marilyn didn't want anyone— not even film extras—to be allowed to have hair as light blond as her own.

Eileen Heckart, the actress who played Vera, was as frustrated as others about Marilyn's lateness and flubbed lines, but she also saw another side: the eternal child who just wanted to play. Eileen's two young boys spent time on the set, and every night, Marilyn would walk onto the balcony with oranges and grapefruits and ask the boys if they wanted to play catch

opposite PLAYING CHERIE IN *BUS STOP*, 1956.

CLOWNING AROUND WITH DON MURRAY
ON THE SET OF *BUS STOP*.

with her, according to their brother Luke Yankee's memoir. Eileen said they had the time of their lives. When she told Marilyn she didn't have to play with them, Marilyn said, "Are you kidding? It's my favorite part of the day! Besides, vitamin C is very important for growing boys. They have to have their citrus!"

Although the two didn't keep in touch, pictures of Marilyn with the boys adorned Eileen's house, and she would often cry when she spoke about Marilyn. "What a sad, lonely young lady. She was adored by millions, but never believed that she was loved."

Having never quite lost his crush on Marilyn, Arthur Miller got into contact with her as soon as he found out she was in New York. Although he was still married, they began a not-very-well-kept secret affair. Each time reporters asked,

Marilyn would vehemently deny the relationship, feigning shock: "How can they say we're having a romance? He's married!" But not for long—he went to Reno for a divorce, which was granted in June 1956. After filming *Bus Stop*, Marilyn came back to New York to be with him.

She was scheduled to leave for London to film *The Prince and the Showgirl* in August, and wanted Arthur to be there with her—but there was a logistical problem. His passport had been revoked due to suspected Communist involvement. He applied for a new one but instead was called to testify before the House Un-American Activities Committee (HUAC). Among other things, they wanted him to name people who were at a Communist meeting with him years earlier. He refused and was declared in contempt of Congress.

Fox wanted Arthur to cooperate with the Committee because of his relationship with Marilyn; any bad press for

above LEFT TO RIGHT: ARTHUR O'CONNELL, EILEEN HECKART, AND MARILYN MONROE IN A STILL FROM *BUS STOP*, 1956.

him could spell bad press for her. Despite studio pressure on Marilyn to get Arthur to give in, she was proud that he wouldn't back down. After his hearing, reporters asked Arthur why he needed the passport in the first place, and he responded that he was going to London to discuss a production of one of his plays, "and I will be there with the woman who will then be my wife." Was there ever a more tantalizing line for the tabloids?

Marilyn would later say that it was unexpected—Arthur hadn't officially proposed before he announced it to the world—but she accepted, and converted to Judaism for him. They soon held a press conference at Arthur's farm in Connecticut so photographers could snap photos of the two of them together, but just before they arrived, there was a car crash, killing one of the reporters. Marilyn was hysterical and thought it was a bad omen, but she soon pulled herself together well.

When asked what kind of wedding they were going to have, Marilyn answered, "Very quiet, I hope."

They refused to give wedding details to the press, but they actually got married later that night in a quick civil ceremony and had a Jewish ceremony two days later at Arthur's agent's home. Lee Strasberg gave the bride away and a small number of friends attended the reception that followed. The normally stoic Arthur was affectionate, enraptured by his new bride, and Marilyn looked very happy.

Like most happiness in Marilyn's life, their newlywed bliss was fleeting. Arthur obtained a limited passport soon after the wedding, and off they went to England together for the filming of *The Prince and the Showgirl*. Marilyn had been so excited to work with costar Laurence Olivier on the film, which was the first true venture of Marilyn Monroe Productions, but their styles clashed badly. It turned into a nightmare for both of them. Laurence would star in the

opposite ARTHUR MILLER AND MARILYN AFTER THEIR CIVIL WEDDING CEREMONY, JUNE 29, 1956. above TOGETHER WITH ARTHUR'S PARENTS ON THE DAY OF THE CEREMONY.

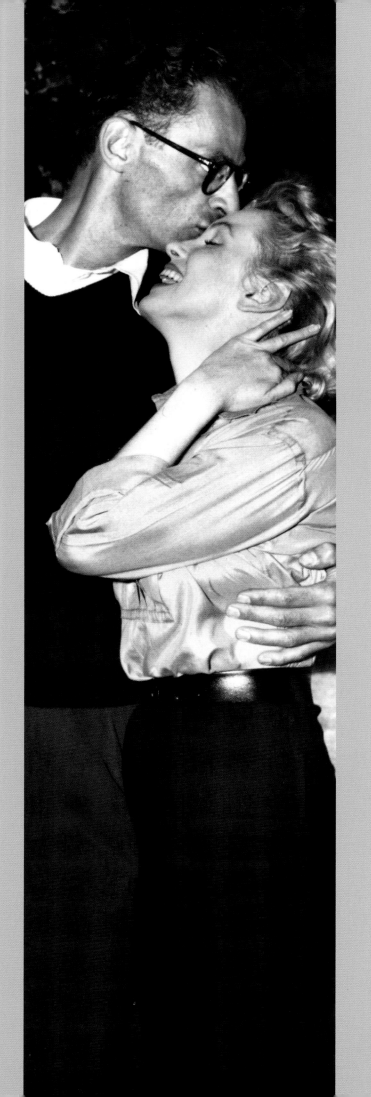

left MARILYN AND ARTHUR ON THE DAY OF THEIR CIVIL WEDDING CEREMONY. opposite THE COUPLE AT THEIR WEDDING RECEPTION.

her first daughter after Marilyn. Costar Richard Wattis came around to liking her, too, though he was at first a little put off by her lateness as well.

But to Marilyn's horror, her husband took Laurence's side. He and Laurence got along very well, to the extent that Laurence eventually pitied Arthur because he felt that Marilyn was stealing all her husband's creative juices. Arthur was no longer writing, Laurence figured, because he was too preoccupied battling Marilyn's demons of insecurity, insomnia, health problems, and pill addiction.

Marilyn found Arthur's notebook open one day to a page where he was writing about his disappointment to discover that he thought he had married an angel, but he had been wrong. In it, he called her a "bitch" or "whore," depending on who she told the story to. The rant compared Marilyn to his first wife, and said that the problems with Laurence were her fault. Arthur apologized and said he had just been letting off steam, but Marilyn never truly forgave this, even though they did move on.

She was upset, too, that Milton seemed to get along with Laurence. It didn't take much to raise Marilyn's distrust and ire. If you talked to her enemy, you became her enemy as well.

Despite the drama behind the scenes, Marilyn was able to solicit some excellent reviews from *The Prince and the Showgirl*. The *Los Angeles Times* reported, "This, I am sure, is Miss Monroe's best cinema effort."

film only if he could also direct and produce, so Marilyn and Milton agreed—before they found out that he was a loud, aggressive director who didn't take well to her lapses of attention and lateness.

The more he yelled, the later she arrived on set—sometimes not showing up at all. Lee's wife, Paula Strasberg, traveled with Marilyn as her personal acting coach, and Laurence hated Paula with a special zeal. He also thought Marilyn was just exaggerating her bouts of endometriosis pain that occurred in relation to her menstrual periods.

Una Pearl, cast as Marilyn's body double, shows that it wasn't all bad on the set, though. "I found her charming, a giggler—the least little thing would set her off laughing," she told journalist Howard Mutti-Mewse. "And she was very down to earth. I didn't find her snooty like some actresses, who wouldn't smile, and would look the other way if you said good morning." Una even named

In February 1957, *Time* reported, "When M-G-M Producer Pandro Berman decided to film Feodor Dostoevsky's *The Brothers Karamazov*, he thought wistfully of blond Cinemactress Marilyn Monroe, who has often confessed a yen to play the role of Grushenka. 'Frankly, I don't expect her to be in it,' he said. 'She would probably want too much money, and besides, I hear she is going to have a baby.' To all questions of diapers and Dostoevsky, Marilyn murmured unsweetened nothings."

above THE COUPLE ARRIVE IN LONDON, JULY 1956. opposite (top) RECEIVING DIRECTION FROM LAURENCE OLIVIER. opposite (bottom) WITH OLIVIER (LEFT) AND MILLER (RIGHT) ATTENDING MILLER'S PLAY "A VIEW FROM THE BRIDGE," LONDON, 1956.

But those nothings were something: Within a few months, she was, indeed, pregnant—a thrill for Marilyn, who had thought it all through before and said, "If I have a little girl, I'll always tell her how pretty she is, and I'll brush her hair until it shines, and I'll never let her alone for a minute." She and Arthur spent the summer in Amagansett, Long Island, where they surfcasted on the beach, tended to the garden, and hosted dinners for Arthur's parents—his mother taught Marilyn how to cook Arthur's favorite meals. When a local woman congratulated Marilyn on her pregnancy and said that she was sewing something special for the baby, Marilyn was so happy she kissed the woman.

It turned out to be an ectopic pregnancy, though, and needed to be terminated to save her life. This was hard on her psyche. Several people who've known her, such as the Strasbergs and the Rostens, said that Marilyn had more than one abortion before this point, and she worried that this was why she couldn't have a baby now. Maybe this was punishment, Marilyn thought.

Despite her desire to have a baby, Marilyn's drinking and sleeping pill–popping habits were getting significantly worse. She began drinking champagne as soon as she awoke, and sometimes lost track of how many pills she took at night or during her bouts with endometriosis. She overdosed and had to be resuscitated more than once.

Arthur began working on the screenplay *The Misfits* to cheer her up. Although he had said earlier that he didn't plan to write anything specifically for Marilyn because he had never been able to write with a particular person in mind before, this was to be his Valentine to her.

Marilyn's relationship with Arthur was up and down: Some people saw them as an adorable couple, while others said they were horrible to each other. Marilyn wound up acting as the breadwinner, even paying Arthur's alimony to his ex-wife, and he charged his new car to Marilyn Monroe Productions.

According to Joshua Greene, Arthur really liked living the high life—spending Marilyn's money on the finest hotels, best champagne, and fanciest cars. Milton tried to point out to Marilyn that Arthur was sucking too much money from the production company's budget, and that if he kept spending, they wouldn't have any profit. Arthur tried to make it sound like Milton was doing the same thing: charging inappropriate things to the company. Not surprisingly, there was a tension between Arthur and the Greenes. It seemed to Milton that Arthur was trying to involve himself in areas he didn't belong.

Joshua remembers, "My father's point of view was, 'Just be her husband. She needs a good husband, lover, and emotional rock. I'll take care of the other stuff.'"

But that's not what happened.

Arthur helped convince Marilyn to ask Milton to give up his partnership in the company. Milton allowed Marilyn to buy him out for only the same amount he had put into the company—he didn't try to make a profit. More than anything, he wanted to show her that he was genuine, and

opposite DURING HER SUMMER IN AMAGANSETT, LONG ISLAND WITH ARTHUR, 1957. above LEAVING THE HOSPITAL WITH ARTHUR AFTER UNDERGOING SURGERY TO END HER ECTOPIC PREGNANCY, AUGUST 1957.

he held out hope until the end that she would stand up for him. He was distraught that he had spent so much effort and money setting up the company, only to be dumped after one production. Moreover, he was devastated to lose his friend, Marilyn, with whom he thought he had such a tight bond. But he knew that Arthur was her husband, which trumped their relationship.

They did not speak again until shortly before her death, when she called out of the blue one day. Then they spoke for three hours, mending their friendship.

It was her first film in almost two years, and people on the set of *Some Like It Hot* in 1958 weren't very happy with Marilyn. Tony Curtis claimed that he and Jack Lemmon were usually on set in costume at 7 a.m., with wig pins sticking into their heads and an inability to go to the bathroom because they were saddled with padding to keep their "you-know-whats" down. Then they'd have to wait for Marilyn, who sometimes wouldn't show until 3 in the afternoon.

Marilyn got pregnant again during filming, and wanted to take it very easy, so Arthur approached director Billy Wilder and said, "Please don't make her *work* before, let's say, 11 o'clock," according to a *Vanity Fair* interview.

"Before 11 o'clock? She's never on the set before 11 o'clock!" Billy responded. "I wish you would be directing it—you would be tearing out your hair, you would slit your own throat, because she's never there! I would be *delighted* if she came after lunch. Every day after lunch? *Please*, I would be delighted to have her."

There was just no rushing her even when she was on set—if an assistant went to fetch her from her dressing room, she was likely to swear at him. Billy called Marilyn "a continuous puzzle without any solution."

And she began to forget even the simplest lines. At one point, the crew taped a piece of paper with the line "Where's that bourbon?" inside every dresser drawer she had to open.

Someone was even paid a weekly salary to hold an umbrella over Marilyn's head to shade her from the sun, Tony

above ARTHUR AND MARILYN IN THEIR CONVERTIBLE WITH MILTON GREENE BY THEIR SIDE. opposite (top) JACK LEMMON (THIRD FROM LEFT) AND MARILYN (FAR RIGHT) JOKE AROUND ON THE SET OF *SOME LIKE IT HOT*, 1959. opposite (bottom) JACK AND MARILYN ON SET.

said. And when she found out they were shooting in black and white because the men's drag makeup looked silly in color, she was furious.

When someone asked what it was like kissing Marilyn in the film, Tony famously responded, "It was like kissing Hitler." Paula Strasberg, who was in the room when he said it, burst into tears and chastised him for saying such a horrible thing. In later years, he vehemently denied having said it, but he clearly admitted it earlier. When British author and former *Ritz* newspaper gossip columnist Frances Lynn asked him about the remark in the 1970s, he said, "What are words? I just wanted to show that she wasn't untouchable. People on the set used to tiptoe 'round the tulips around her."

At least the musicians liked her. Robert F. Robinson, a trombonist, played on Marilyn's song "Running Wild." He says, "She was very shy and really very nice. She was supposed to record the song with us, but it took all day and she didn't get one take right in all of it. It wasn't always her fault,

but something always happened. So they recorded with the orchestra and they brought her in the next day to dub her voice in, and she did a very good job." He said that everyone in the orchestra enjoyed meeting her—"You could be with her and not even know she's Marilyn Monroe."

Despite taking it easy, Marilyn had a miscarriage toward the end of shooting, and was miserable. She would later have an elective surgery to improve her odds of carrying a baby, but to no avail. By the end of this film, she and the people around her were drained, and Billy vowed not to work with her again.

Looking back many years later, he compared working with her to going to the dentist: "It was hell at the time, but after it was over, it was wonderful." And indeed, it's hard to detect any tension in the film: It remains a classic comedy where Marilyn's talents shine.

Despite positive reviews, Marilyn wasn't happy with *Some Like It Hot*. She thought she looked fat, and she felt it

above GENE KELLY (CENTER) WORKING WITH YVES MONTAND (RIGHT) AND MARILYN MONROE ON THE SET OF *LET'S MAKE LOVE*, 1959.

represented the low expectations people had about her acting. "If I were a car, they'd be driving me in low gear. That's bad for the engine and depressing for the car, you know what I mean?" she said to Lee Strasberg.

To fulfill her contractual obligation, Marilyn accepted Fox's *Let's Make Love* project, despite her concern that the script was lousy. Arthur rewrote it to improve Marilyn's part, but it remained a pretty pointless film. But its significance in Marilyn's life is due to the antics that went on behind the camera.

Yves Montand played the male lead; he and his wife, Simone Signoret, quickly befriended Marilyn and Arthur. But when Arthur went back to New York and Simone went back to Paris, Marilyn went to Yves's room with nothing but a mink coat on.

They made very little effort to conceal their affair; they were seen together in cars and around town, staring longingly at each other at press conferences, drinking champagne together . . . though they both strongly denied romance at first. Instead, they focused on praising each other's talents, with Yves saying, "Marilyn is certainly one, if not *the* greatest actress I have ever worked with."

A waiter at the Beverly Hills Hotel served the two breakfast in bed and reported back to Associated Press columnist James Bacon that they were naked. James was a friend of Marilyn's, and decided to mess with her a bit, even though he didn't plan to print the story. He called the room and asked Yves what he was doing naked in bed with Marilyn Monroe. "I next heard a voice speaking French so fast that I doubt any native Parisian could have kept up with it," James later wrote in *Beverly Hills 213 Magazine*. "I then hung up. A half hour later, Marilyn's publicist called and said: 'Yves and Marilyn were merely rehearsing their lines for the movie.' I answered with one word: 'Naked?' That ended that conversation. A few days later, I saw Marilyn on the Fox lot. She smiled and said 'You devil, you.' I smiled back."

Yves's wife gave a good act in public, pretending not to care or not to believe what was happening. She said that if Marilyn was in love with her husband, it only proved that she had good taste. But in private, although they remained married, Simone moved out of the bedroom and stopped sleeping with her husband.

Before shooting began in Reno, director John Huston said, "I gave Marilyn her first big break in *The Asphalt Jungle*. There won't be any trouble on *The Misfits*, I guarantee you. Her husband wrote it, and I have his support!"

Little did he know.

At long last, Marilyn was working with a hero of hers, Clark Gable. And with her old friend Eli Wallach and new confidant Montgomery Clift, an actor who Marilyn once described as "the only person I know who's in worse shape than I am." And her production company was coproducing the film, which had been written for her by her husband—it all sounded like ideal circumstances for Marilyn, yet she spiraled quickly downward. Production manager C. O. "Doc"

above IN THE RECORDING STUDIO, LISTENING TO PLAYBACK OF "MY HEART BELONGS TO DADDY" FOR THE FILM *LET'S MAKE LOVE.*

Arthur approached John and Doc and told them that Marilyn needed to go to Los Angeles to get treatment. The film shut down for a week, and the official explanation was that Marilyn was "exhausted." Doc says there were no thoughts of firing her, but there were quiet discussions: "What are we going to do if she can't come back?"

When she did come back, though, Doc says she seemed refreshed. He remembers running into Marilyn and Arthur taking a walk by the river, and thinking they looked good. But that wasn't to last either. When the studio doctor wouldn't give her any more pills, she found a local doctor who would.

Director John Huston had a birthday party during filming, and comedian Mort Sahl entertained. "Huston was drunk, and he introduced me to Marilyn, whom I'd known for years," he wrote in *Heartland*. "And she was drunk, and she took my hand and put it right on her breast and she said, 'Don't be afraid, Mr. Sahl.' And I said, 'I'm not afraid.' And she said, 'How wrong you are. We're all afraid.' "

"Marilyn's moods shifted like clouds passing across the sun," said photographer Eve Arnold. Marilyn began to hate her part in the film and hate Arthur for writing it for her. Several people noted that she was unnecessarily cruel to Arthur, attempting to belittle and humiliate him at every turn. The crew sometimes heard them fighting in the hotel. Eventually, they got separate hotel rooms.

"I was not at first aware that she and Arthur had virtually separated, but when he asked if he could come in the car with John and me, of course I said 'yes,' " says script supervisor Angela Allen. "He was banned, evidently, from her car. Only Paula [Strasberg] and possibly some of her multiple entourage traveled with her."

Angela also helped Arthur by typing up his rewrite notes. Marilyn grew convinced that Arthur was having an affair with Angela, which wasn't true. She also turned on Eli Wallach for a very flimsy reason: She thought he had purposely upstaged her in a dance scene. Although Marilyn

Erickson took on the task of making sure Marilyn made it from the hotel to the set each day, but she was often hours and hours late. Some days, the hair or makeup people would tell Doc that she was on her way down, so he'd leave for the set, figuring she was right behind him—but an hour later, she still would be dallying in her hotel room.

Some thought she had good reason to put off her appearance on set—the cast and crew quickly agreed that she was in no condition to perform. Doc observed that "it was because of the medications she was taking. She couldn't sleep, so she would take a lot of sleeping pills, and she couldn't get up in the morning to get going again, so she would need stimulants to get her out and about. The combination of things finally wore her out and she was in pretty bad shape."

Insomnia was a major problem throughout most of Marilyn's career. One thing that helped was massage, so she enlisted the help of her trusted friend and masseuse Ralph L. Roberts, who made himself available to her literally around the clock. She would often call in the middle of the night, and he'd rush over to soothe her back to sleep, for about $25 per massage. He cared deeply about Marilyn and didn't mind listening as she talked about her troubles again and again.

above WITH YVES MONTAND (RIGHT) AT A 20TH CENTURY FOX LUNCHEON. opposite (top) WITH JOHN HUSTON (LEFT) AND MILLER (RIGHT) ON LOCATION IN RENO, NEVADA, 1961. opposite (bottom) WITH MILLER ON A BREAK FOR *THE MISFITS*.

had been close to the whole Wallach family when she first arrived in New York, things were different now. "My son was eager to see Marilyn, whom he hadn't seen since she had babysat him, and show her his costume," Eli says in his memoir. "But the moment we got to her trailer, she looked out and when she saw us, she shut the door."

Eli was impressed that Clark Gable was always so patient with Marilyn. Whenever she showed up, Clark would greet her with hugs and compliments about the scenes she had done with him. Clark told Eli that he was afraid that if he chastised her, "It would only deepen her despair."

Masseuse Ralph Roberts remembered that Clark once came to Marilyn's room and said, "Marilyn, I have to tell you that I've had reservations about you and your temperament. I wanted to do this picture more than I can tell you, and even if it meant working with you, I was determined to do

it. As far as I can see, you're about the least temperamental person involved." She was thrilled to hear him say it.

Just days after *The Misfits* wrapped, though, Clark died of a heart attack. No one had even known he had a heart condition. Gossip turned to Marilyn; reports said that pregnant widow Kay Gable blamed Marilyn for putting tremendous strain on Clark, making him wait for her in heat that reached up to 108 degrees day after day. The news of Clark's death came at the same time Marilyn and Arthur announced their separation.

Marilyn was barely coherent. She began seeing psychiatrist Dr. Ralph Greenson at his office every afternoon.

Marilyn's unpredictable moods and psychological problems caused those around her to have strongly conflicting impressions of her—those who met her on a good day thought she

above SHIELDING HERSELF FROM THE DESERT SUN ON THE SET OF *THE MISFITS*, 1961.

was bubbly and sweet, and some who met her on bad days thought she was self-centered and even cruel. Though he met her only twice, Douglas Kirkland got to see both sides.

Douglas was a new celebrity photographer for *Look* magazine when he was assigned to photograph Marilyn in her apartment. "It was so modest, like a hotel room or something," he says. Not like a movie star's home.

As usual, she was extraordinarily late, but he was so dazzled by the sight of this angel breezing in that he forgot to be upset. They got to work, and the atmosphere got more sexual as she stripped nude under her bedsheets. She asked everyone but Douglas to leave the room. He photographed her from above the bed, and she stopped and asked, "Why don't you come down here with me?"

"I didn't really acknowledge that I understood," he says. "I didn't say no, but at the same time, I just sort of smiled in a very boyish way. I never knew at that time if I did the right thing or not. Ultimately, I think I did, but at that moment, I was disturbed with myself. I felt I wasn't a real man. Any

real man would have jumped in that bed, and I was certainly ready, but something stopped me: the combination of my family, and also wanting to do the work."

Marilyn loved cameras and photographers, and Douglas says she loved inventing her own roles. Her insecurities, crippling on movie sets, never showed on photo sessions, and he believes that this was because "She could respond to the individual behind the camera, whereas on a movie, the script is written and she has to play a role. It's all blocked out. With the still camera, she could just talk back to you."

After the shoot, they had an intimate conversation about their backgrounds and ambitions, and Douglas left with a wonderful feeling about her. That's why it was so jarring when he came back to show her the shots and she was cold and rude to him.

"She was very depressed. I have no idea what dark things had happened," he says. But she quickly began cutting up almost half of the two hundred and forty or so pictures he took, and marking others out with a grease

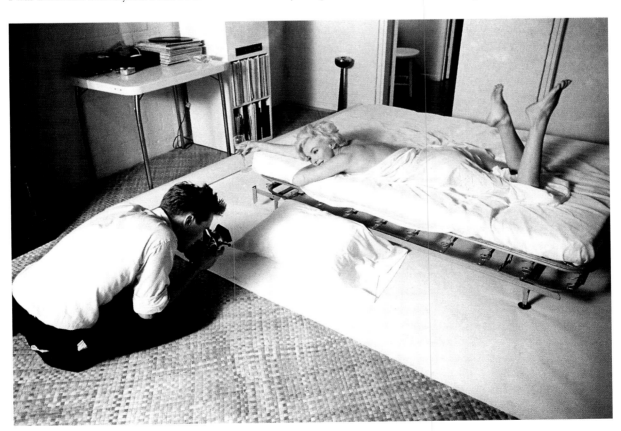

above PHOTOGRAPHER DOUGLAS KIRKLAND SHOOTS MARILYN WRAPPED IN NOTHING BUT A WHITE BED SHEET.

pencil. Eventually, she found some she liked a lot, and she softened a bit. But Douglas still felt as if he'd been with an entirely different person from the glowing, sexually charged sweetheart he'd met the previous night.

Marilyn began seeing Joe DiMaggio again, but apparently didn't expect to reconcile with him. This didn't stop gossip about remarriage, though. At the 33rd Annual Academy Awards, Bob Hope even dedicated "Best Song" nominee "The Second Time Around" to Marilyn and Joe. Were it up to Joe, there probably would have been a second marriage; he told friends he planned to ask her again, but her friends didn't believe she would say yes. Joe proved to be a much better friend than husband, however, giving her as much support as he could.

Shortly after a trip to Mexico to get a fast divorce in 1961, Marilyn entered the Payne-Whitney Clinic at the suggestion of one of her psychiatrists. But she wasn't expecting the atmosphere she found there at all—bars on the windows, locked rooms, no privacy. And once she was in, they wouldn't let her out without her psychiatrist's order. She became extremely agitated, throwing a chair at a window and threatening to cut herself with the broken glass. It was her terror come true: She had always feared she'd end up locked in a mental institution, "going crazy" like her mother and so many others in her family.

A letter she sent to the Strasbergs said, "I'm locked up with these poor nutty people. I'm sure to end up a nut too if I stay in this nightmare. Please help me." But they couldn't, so she begged Joe DiMaggio to get her out of there. He did, threatening to take the place down "brick by brick" if the psychiatrist didn't comply. They transferred her to Columbia-Presbyterian Medical Center instead, where she stayed for three weeks.

Marlon Brando, her friend and likely an occasional lover, sent Marilyn a telegram while she was there: "The best reappraisals are born in the worst crisis. It has happened

to all of us in relative degrees. Be glad for it and don't be afraid of it. It can only help. Relax and enjoy it. I send you my thoughts and my warmest affections. Marlon."

On her release, she sat next to Arthur at his mother's funeral. Shortly afterward, she flew to Florida to recuperate with Joe and visit with her half-sister, Berniece. Frank Sinatra gave her a white poodle to replace the basset hound she lost in the divorce from Arthur. She named the poodle "Maf," short for "mafia."

Despite this proof that she had people who cared about her, when a reporter asked if she was going to have a birthday party that year, she said, "I'd love to have a party, but I have no friends."

A host of physical problems followed the psychological ones, and Marilyn was in and out of hospitals for more gynecological surgery and a gallbladder operation. It would be a full year before she set foot on a film set again, and when she did, it was disastrous.

opposite A DOUGLAS KIRKLAND PHOTO. above MARILYN AND JOE RETURN TO NEW YORK FROM THEIR VACATION IN TAMPA, FLORIDA, APRIL 1961.

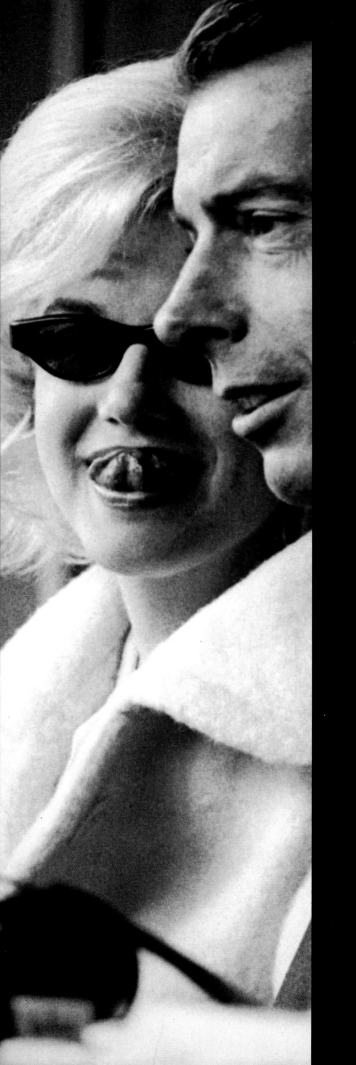

left MARILYN AND DIMAGGIO ATTE[N]
OPENING GAME AT YANKEE STADIU[M]
1961. opposite CUDDLING HER POOD[LE]
AT THE BEVERLY HILLS HOTEL, 1961.

CHAPTER NINE

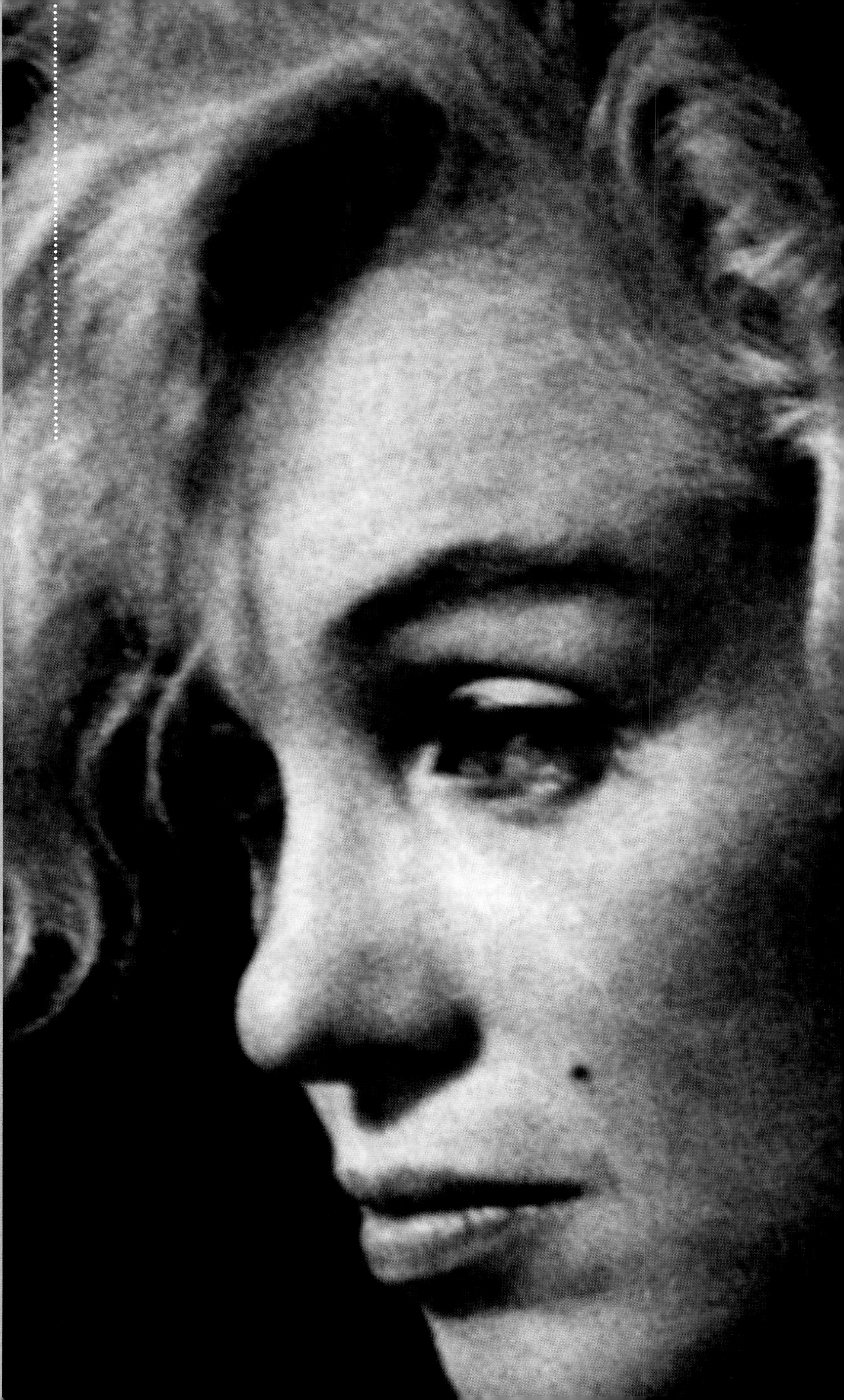

INCOMPLETE

"I FEEL AS THOUGH IT'S ALL HAPPENING TO SOMEONE RIGHT NEXT TO ME. I'M CLOSE, I CAN FEEL IT, I CAN HEAR IT, BUT IT ISN'T REALLY ME."

Her psychiatrist, Dr. Greenson, recommended that getting back to work would be good for her. But on the first day of *Something's Got to Give* in April 1962, she called in sick with a sinus infection. Although the studio doctor wanted to postpone the filming, director George Cukor and Fox executives decided to press forward. But Marilyn rarely showed up, and they believed she was exaggerating her illness.

Prior to the film's start, Marilyn had received permission from Fox to take time off to attend President Kennedy's birthday party, but after a month of illness and delays, no one thought she would still expect to go—the studio was losing money every day she wasn't there, and filming was significantly behind schedule. But she did go, singing her famous "Happy Birthday" rendition to the President, infuriating Fox executives who were now convinced she had been faking her illness.

In his biography of Robert Kennedy, Arthur M. Schlesinger Jr. writes of that night, "I do not think I have ever seen anyone so beautiful; I was enchanted by her manner and her wit, at once so masked, so ingenuous, and so penetrating. But one felt a terrible unreality about her—as if talking to someone under water."

That could well have been because she was drunk and feverish. She collapsed backstage, but put herself together for the after-party, where people remarked that Bobby Kennedy wanted all her attention. Afterward Ralph Roberts massaged her to sleep until about 4 a.m.,

opposite PORTRAIT TAKEN AT A HOLLYWOOD PARTY IN JANUARY 1962.

disproving the rumors that she sneaked off to a hotel with John F. Kennedy that night.

When she came back to the set of *Something's Got to Give* in late May, she briefly won everyone's good graces again by doing a nude swimming scene and letting photographers capture it for publicity shots. She had lost weight after her recent gallbladder surgery, and she looked terrific. She had been determined to oust Elizabeth Taylor (who was working on *Cleopatra*) from magazine covers, and she succeeded. Soon, Marilyn's face was all over the newsstand, leaving Elizabeth in her shadow.

But her return to work didn't last long; her birthday, June 1, would be her last day on set. Her stand-in, Evelyn Moriarty, bought her a birthday cake, which George Cukor insisted not be brought out until he had gotten a full day's work out of Marilyn. That night, she went to Dodger Stadium for a muscular dystrophy fund-raiser, then called in sick with a fever the next day. That was the last straw; she had attended only thirteen out of thirty days of work, and

Fox decided they weren't going to take it anymore. They fired her.

Lee Remick was to replace her, but Dean Martin refused to work with anyone but Marilyn. Fox tried to sue him for $3 million for breach of contract. Marilyn was thrilled that he stood up for her in this way, and she wanted to get back to work. While talks with the studio were under way, she turned down an invitation to a dinner party from Mr. and Mrs. Bobby Kennedy. Her telegram read, "Unfortunately, I am involved in a freedom ride protesting the loss of the minority rights belonging to the few remaining earthbound stars. All we demanded was our right to twinkle."

Despite all the venom, after cooler heads prevailed, Fox re-hired Marilyn for more money than they originally contracted. The shoot was to resume in October 1962.

She had two more films to complete after *Something's Got to Give* to finish out her Fox contract. The next project she was considering was *The Stripper*, a film adaptation of the play *A*

opposite (top and bottom) SWIMMING NUDE FOR THE POOL SCENE IN *SOMETHING'S GOT TO GIVE*, 1962. above DIRECTOR GEORGE CUKOR PRESENTS MARILYN WITH A BIRTHDAY CAKE AT THE END OF A DAY OF FILMING.

Loss of Roses. Playwright William Inge had written the role of Lila with Marilyn in mind, though she couldn't handle the stress of doing a live stage play. When it was rewritten for film, however, Marilyn met with filmmakers Jerry Wald and Curtis Harrington, telling them her ideas for the part. She particularly loved two scenes of Lila's: one endearing one with the male lead, and a dramatic scene where she attempts suicide with broken glass.

John Gilmore, author of *Inside Marilyn Monroe*, had the male lead role in the play and was up for the same part in the film. Curtis showed him script revisions, saying, "Whatever you do, do not show it to Marilyn."

"I immediately called her and said, 'I got the script. You might not really like it, though,'" he says. When she came to his apartment and read it, John remembers, "She was very hurt. They chopped up the scene with the boy and cut out the entire suicide scene that she was so excited to do. She tore the pages out of the script and she put them in the fireplace, and then she took a match and lit it. She took pills and told me it was medication. Then she was in my bathroom for a real long time; I think she was taking more pills."

It's interesting that Marilyn was drawn to the suicide scene; in prior films, she was seemingly personally offended whenever a character of hers showed any sign of mental illness, or even extreme anger. She absolutely hated the scene in *The Misfits* where her character screamed about the treatment of the horses, despite the fact that it became one of the film's most memorable scenes. It was as if showing these sides of her characters would expose that she, too, had these feelings. Yet at the same time, she desperately wanted to play roles with depth.

She and John went to dinner at Ernie's restaurant, where she had bacon and asparagus with water, and another pill "for dessert." She wore a big black scarf and glasses, but the waiter still recognized her—his hands shook as he served them.

Back at John's apartment, Marilyn looked into the thermos she had brought and found the remains of a margarita. "I don't know how long it has been in here," she said. "The salt will preserve it—don't you think?" They shared it, then John walked her to her car.

"She looked really bothered. I bent down to the window, and said, 'Are you all right?' She said, 'Yes. Ciao. Ciao.' She took off and that was the last I ever saw her."

"The public was the only family, only Prince Charming, and only home I had ever dreamed about," Marilyn once said. But in the summer of 1962, she needed something more than "the public."

She had been looking for love again, and having reckless affairs—with singers, writers, photographers . . . and at least one politician. "She would sit on the floor at his knees and just gaze up at Jack Kennedy, listening to every single word he said," says Nancy Bacon. "She loved smart people. She was always trying to learn and absorb their intelligence."

Just about anyone who knew her will tell you that, yes, she had an affair with John F. Kennedy. How serious that affair was is up for debate; some say she honestly thought he

DANCING WITH MARTINI IN HAND
AT PRODUCER HENRY WEINSTEIN'S
HOLLYWOOD HOME IN JANUARY 1962.

left and opposite SINGING "HAPPY BIRTHDAY" TO PRESIDENT KENNEDY AT HIS BIRTHDAY CELEBRATION.

would leave his wife and that she'd become the First Lady, but Lee and Paula's daughter Susan Strasberg said that Marilyn had no such thoughts: "It was okay for one night to sleep with a charismatic President—and she loved the secrecy and drama of it. But he certainly wasn't the kind of man she wanted for life, and she was very clear to us about this."

The only verifiable time the two slept together was at a party at Bing Crosby's house. From there, she called Ralph, her friend and masseur, and put President Kennedy on the phone to ask for advice about his back troubles. She later told friends that he was bad in bed.

Still, when President Kennedy's private phone number changed and he didn't give it to her, she apparently made a big fuss to the White House switchboard operators. Bobby Kennedy asked her to stop trying to reach his brother. Then the gossip takes a different turn: Did the President "pass" her to his brother? Did she fall in love with Bobby?

Phone records show that Marilyn made many phone calls to Bobby's office that summer, but Bobby's press aide

Ed Guthman says that was no proof of an affair—many celebrities called Bobby because he was a good listener. And Ralph said that Marilyn told him she wasn't physically attracted to Bobby.

Actress Mamie Van Doren, who was an acquaintance of Marilyn's since her early years as a model, agrees. "She didn't even like Bobby. He gave her a bad time; he was the go-between. It was always JFK—she was crazy about Jack. She's not about to marry an attorney general. She went for the pres, honey!"

"Don't ever fall in love with a politician. When they fuck you, they fuck you," Marilyn told her.

When an acquaintance asked Ralph Roberts what Marilyn was like, he said, "Like almost everyone I know—especially women—in the theater. There's a motor continually going. But I think when she gets depressed she gets more so than any of you. She withdraws more; she'll go into that darkened bedroom and stay for days. She's more moody than anyone

above ACTRESS MAMIE VAN DOREN WITH HER SON, PERRY RAY ANTHONY, IN 1958.

I've ever known. She uses the word 'blue' often to describe how she feels, and it seems to me that it's the darkest shade of blue one can possibly imagine. I've seen all of you in the depths, but I believe she has devils to accompany her. On the other hand, I've laughed more with her than I think I ever have with anyone."

Marilyn was seeing psychiatrist Ralph Greenson on a daily basis just to get through each week. With his encouragement, she bought her first home on Fifth Helena Drive in Los Angeles. It meant a lot to her to have a place that was really hers. Greenson sent Eunice Murray to become Marilyn's housekeeper, but many believe her real position was more like "spy." She reported back to Greenson about Marilyn's activities. Greenson also tried to cut Marilyn off from her friends, whom he deemed bad influences.

Ralph Roberts had a key so he could come in whenever Marilyn needed help falling asleep, and leave without waking her, but even he was one of Greenson's targets. For the most part, Marilyn went along with whatever Greenson told her to do. Maybe she trusted him to run her life better than she could herself.

Along with her hairdresser, Eunice, and her publicist, Marilyn went to Mexico to buy furnishings to decorate her new home—just like Greenson's own Mexican-styled house. While there she met writer José Bolaños, who came back to Los Angeles to escort Marilyn to the Golden Globe Awards, where she won female World Film Favorite.

Marilyn had hunches, but she probably didn't realize that the FBI was tracking her closely since her relationship with Arthur Miller—their first reports indicate that Marilyn sought a visa to the U.S.S.R. in 1955—and that they were particularly interested in this trip, where she met up with expatriate American Communists and apparently discussed things John F. Kennedy and Bobby Kennedy had told her. Her house was bugged, too, though it's not clear who was on

above MARILYN WITH WRITER JOSÉ BOLAÑOS, HER DATE TO THE 1962 GOLDEN GLOBES.

the receiving end: private detectives, the FBI, or the mafia—or all three. A later tenant of her home paid a contractor to remove wiring from the house and roof that was consistent with the wiring used for bugging devices.

Soon after her visit to Mexico, Marilyn met up with Mamie Van Doren by chance at the Russian Tea Room, and they sat and talked.

Mamie remembers, "I was working in the theater at the time, and she said, 'How do you get up in front of an audience and remember all those lines? I couldn't do it.' Then she asked me about my kid. She said she just got back from Mexico, and she was thinking about adopting, but in those days it was really hard—she couldn't get adoption rights. She wanted to get married and have a family and have a normal life. She just didn't pick the right guys."

Marilyn looked haggard, says Mamie, and it was clear she was on a downward spiral. "It was just rejection," says Mamie. "She couldn't handle rejection."

Knowing that Marilyn was in trouble, Frank Sinatra invited her to visit the Cal-Neva Lodge, which he owned. After his private jet picked up Marilyn, the pilot went for President Kennedy's brother-in-law and "Rat Pack" member Peter Lawford, who had remained a friend of Marilyn's since they dated early in her career. What happened there is a mystery, although everyone who saw her that week said she was clearly a wreck, lost in a haze of alcohol and pills.

James Gray-Gold, son of baseball manager "Lefty" O'Doul, worked as a parking attendant at the Cal-Neva. As a young boy, he knew Marilyn through his parents' friendship with Joe DiMaggio, and when he saw Marilyn emerge from her car, he was saddened to see that her "glow was now a glimmer."

On August 2, according to James's article in *Hollywood Nostalgia*, she approached him in the casino. It was a warm day, but, not for the first time in her life, Marilyn was wearing her full-length mink coat with nothing underneath.

above WITH PETER LAWFORD AT THE CAL-NEVA LODGE, 1962. opposite (top) WITH CELEBRITY FRIENDS AT THE LODGE. opposite (bottom) LEFT TO RIGHT: PETER LAWFORD, MAY BRITT, FRANK SINATRA, AND MARILYN MONROE.

"Her gait was halting as she threw her arms around my neck and kissed me. 'Jimmy, Wingy [Grover, a casino boss] just told me you were working here. Why haven't you come to see me? I've been here for a week!' Actually, she'd been there four days, but she wasn't in any condition to count the days. I told her I had wanted to see her, but 'security had seemed a bit severe.' Marilyn didn't speak for the longest time, then she looked at me sadly and said, 'Well, anyway, we're here now.' We spoke about my mother, Joe D., and about the last time we had seen each other. She couldn't have been sweeter. It made me very sad to see her so disheveled and unhappy."

He promised to stop by her room to see her later that night, then bodyguard Ed Pucci escorted her away. "She looked back at me. She seemed so alone. These people, I thought, were not her friends. They were jaded men just using her. I went back later that night, but Marilyn had overdosed on Nembutal and was under the house doctor's care in secret."

Many books and documentaries have attempted to uncover the truth about how Marilyn died. Despite exhaustive efforts, the researchers disagree about whether it was suicide, accidental overdose, or murder—and if murder, by whom and why?

The bare facts are these: Publicist Pat Newcomb had slept over and argued with Marilyn in the morning. Marilyn was unable to sleep and was irritated to see Pat so perky, she said. Then Ralph Greenson came over for a psychiatric session that lasted several hours. Joe DiMaggio Jr. called and told Marilyn he had broken up with his fiancée, which was great news to Marilyn since she didn't like the woman. Marilyn called Greenson to share the good news. She also made several other calls that evening—an astonishing number of people claim to have spoken with her during the hours before her death, but the phone records have disappeared.

Peter Lawford invited Marilyn to a party that night, but she turned down the invitation. When he called back later, he became concerned about her slurred speech and unresponsiveness. According to Peter, at the end of the call, she said, "Say good-bye to Pat, say good-bye to Jack, and say good-bye to yourself because you're a nice guy." When he tried calling back, the line was busy, so he called his agent, who then called Marilyn's lawyer, Milton Rudin (who was also Ralph Greenson's brother-in-law). Milton called the house to check on Marilyn, and housekeeper Eunice said she had just looked in on Marilyn and all was well. Ralph had given her a sedative, she said.

Eunice said she awoke around 3 a.m. and saw a light under Marilyn's door. She tried to get in to check on her, but the bedroom door was locked. She went outside and saw through a window that Marilyn was immobile, so she called Ralph Greenson, who broke in through the window and discovered that Marilyn was dead. Then they called Dr. Hyman Engleberg to the scene.

When police arrived, Eunice was doing laundry, oddly enough. One officer wrote in his report, "It is officer's opinion that Mrs. Murray was vague and possibly evasive in answering questions pertaining to the activities of Miss Monroe during this time."

Eunice's story about finding Marilyn at 3 a.m. had to have been wrong, considering that several people had already been notified of her death before midnight. Why had no one called the police for so long? Unbelievably, they claimed they were waiting for the Fox publicity department to approve the call.

Morticians estimated her time of death between 9:30 and 11:30 p.m. on August 4, even though she was not officially declared dead until the morning of August 5. Her death was termed a "probable suicide."

"She was on her side. It seemed to me . . . put it to you this way, I could stand across the room and tell that she was dead," Hyman told investigators.

opposite (top) MARILYN'S BEDROOM WINDOW, BROKEN BY RALPH GREENSON. opposite (bottom) POLICE CONDUCT AN INVESTIGATION OF THE ROOM WHERE MARILYN DIED, AUGUST 1962.

She died of an overdose of Nembutal, combined with chloral hydrate, but it's unlikely she took the pills orally. There was no pill residue in her stomach, which means either it was all fully metabolized very quickly, or the drug entered her system in another manner. An injection is also unlikely, because it would have killed her almost instantly, not allowed her time to make many phone calls. A likely method is by enema, but if that's the case, it's not clear whether she gave it to herself or (as many suspect) Eunice administered it.

It's obvious there was a cover-up following Marilyn's death. Stories kept changing, evidence disappeared, her body appeared to have been placed in its position clutching the phone. In a 1985 interview for the documentary *Say Goodbye to the President*, Eunice said after the camera stopped rolling, "Why, at my age, do I still have to cover up this thing?"

Of course the question, which has yet to be answered, is why a cover-up was necessary.

Eunice said that Robert Kennedy was at the house that day, and that a doctor and ambulance had come for Marilyn while she was still alive. But her credibility is so low that it's hard to trust anything she said.

The cover-up could have been due to doctor errors: Perhaps the doctors didn't want anyone to discover that they had accidentally given her too many drugs, or that they had prescribed things that were dangerous in combination. Perhaps the cover-up was to protect the President and attorney general, to eliminate any evidence that they saw Marilyn socially or told her secret information. Covering up an affair is not the same as covering up murder—which is still a separate possibility.

The investigation into Marilyn's death was reopened in 1982, concluding that there was no evidence of murder. Efforts to have the case reopened again in 1986 failed.

Try as they might, film studios never did find "the next Marilyn Monroe." Aside from her acting talents and her

above MARILYN'S CASKET PROCESSING OUT OF THE WESTWOOD PARK CHAPEL PAST A LINE OF GUARDS AFTER HER FUNERAL.

MARILYN MONROE
1926 — 1962

MARILYN MONROE'S TOMB,
ADORNED THREE TIMES A WEEK
FOR TWENTY YEARS WITH ROSES
FROM JOE DIMAGGIO.

beauty, there was a quality about her that couldn't be imitated: her spirit. Insecure, needy, loving, passionate, ambitious, always searching within herself for something great . . . looking at Marilyn is like looking into a reflecting pool. She represents qualities in each of us, and in people we love. And there's something so heartbreaking about the knowledge that the world's most everlasting star died alone, achieving so much and yet not reaching the dreams she wanted most.

For twenty years, a local florist delivered roses to Marilyn's crypt three times a week from Joe DiMaggio, a promise he made when they married. After her body lay unclaimed for hours, he was the one who claimed her and made the funeral arrangements, with the help of Berniece Miracle and business manager Inez Melson—very specifically barring her Hollywood friends and the Kennedys, all of whom he thought bore moral responsibility for her death. "I love you, I love you, I love you," he said as he leaned over her casket. Joe never remarried.

Knowing how much it meant to her to put her handprints in the cement at Grauman's Chinese Theatre, imagine what it would mean to her if she knew that her image would be one of the world's most recognizable close to fifty years after her death. No actress has ever surpassed Marilyn's fame.

"If I am a star, the people made me a star," said Marilyn. "No studio, no person, but the people did."

above MARILYN'S HANDPRINTS IN THE CEMENT OUTSIDE GRAUMAN'S CHINESE THEATRE. opposite HER FAVORITE IMAGE OF HERSELF, TAKEN BY CECIL BEATON, 1956.

FILMOGRAPHY

All dates listed below are release dates.

The Shocking Miss Pilgrim (1947)
20th Century Fox
Directed By: George Seaton
Starring: Betty Grable, Dick Haymes
Role: Telephone Operator (uncredited)

Dangerous Years (1947)
20th Century Fox
Directed By: Arthur Pierson
Starring: Billy Halop, Ann E. Todd
Role: Evie

Scudda Hoo! Scudda Hay! (1948)
20th Century Fox
Directed By: F. Hugh Herbert
Starring: June Haver and Lon McCallister
Role: Girl in Canoe

Green Grass of Wyoming (1948)
20th Century Fox
Directed By: Louis King
Starring: Peggy Cummins and Charles Coburn
Role: Extra at square dance (uncredited)

Ladies of the Chorus (1948)
Columbia Pictures
Directed By: Phil Karlson
Role: Peggy Martin

Love Happy (1949)
United Artists
Directed By: David Miller
Starring: Harpo Marx, Chico Marx, Groucho Marx
Role: Grunion's Client

A Ticket to Tomahawk (1950)
20th Century Fox
Directed By: Richard Sale
Starring: Dan Dailey, Anne Baxter
Role: Clara (uncredited)

The Asphalt Jungle (1950)
Metro-Goldwyn-Mayer
Directed By: John Huston
Starring: Sterling Hayden, Louis Calhern
Role: Angela Phinlay

The Fireball (1950)
Bert E. Friedlob Productions
Directed By: Tay Garnett
Starring: Mickey Rooney, Pat O'Brien
Role: Polly

All About Eve (1950)
20th Century Fox
Directed By: Joseph L. Mankiewicz
Starring: Bette Davis
Role: Miss Casswell

left FILMING A TAKE OF *THE PRINCE AND THE SHOWGIRL*, ORIGINALLY TITLED *THE SLEEPING PRINCE*, AUGUST 1956. page 176 BLOWING A KISS, 1956.

Right Cross (1950)
Metro-Goldwyn-Mayer
Directed By: John Sturges
Starring: June Allyson, Dick Powell, Ricardo Montalban
Role: Dusky Ledoux (uncredited)

Home Town Story (1951)
Metro-Goldwyn-Mayer
Directed By: Arthur Pierson
Starring: Jeffrey Lynn, Donald Crisp
Role: Iris Martin

As Young as You Feel (1951)
20th Century Fox
Directed By: Harmon Jones
Starring: Thelma Ritter, Constance Bennett
Role: Harriet

Love Nest (1951)
20th Century Fox
Directed By: Joseph M. Newman
Starring: June Haver, William Lundigan
Role: Roberta 'Bobbie' Stevens

Let's Make It Legal (1951)
20th Century Fox
Directed By: Richard Sale
Starring: Claudette Colbert, Macdonald Carey
Role: Joyce Mannering

Clash by Night (1952)
RKO Radio Pictures
Directed By: Fritz Lang
Starring: Barbara Stanwyck, Paul Douglas
Role: Peggy

We're Not Married! (1952)
20th Century Fox
Directed By: Edmund Goulding
Starring: Ginger Rogers, Fred Allen
Role: Annabel Jones Norris

Don't Bother to Knock (1952)
20th Century Fox
Directed By: Roy Ward Baker
Starring: Richard Widmark
Role: Nell Forbes

Monkey Business (1952)
20th Century Fox
Directed By: Howard Hawks
Starring: Cary Grant, Ginger Rogers, Charles Coburn
Role: Miss Lois Laurel

O. Henry's Full House (1952)
20th Century Fox
Directed By: Henry Hathaway, Howard Hawks, Henry King, Henry Koster, Jean Negulesco
Starring: Charles Laughton, David Wayne
Role: Streetwalker (The Cop and the Anthem)

Niagara (1953)
20th Century Fox
Directed By: Henry Hathaway
Starring: Joseph Cotton, Jean Peters
Role: Rose Loomis

Gentlemen Prefer Blondes (1953)
20th Century Fox
Directed By: Howard Hawks
Starring: Jane Russell
Role: Lorelei Lee

How to Marry a Millionaire (1953)
20th Century Fox
Directed By: Jean Negulesco
Starring: Lauren Bacall, Betty Grable
Role: Pola Debevoise

River of No Return (1954)
20th Century Fox
Directed By: Otto Preminger
Starring: Robert Mitchum, Rory Calhoun
Role: Kay Weston

There's No Business Like Show Business (1954)
20th Century Fox
Directed By: Walter Lang
Starring: Ethel Merman, Donald O'Connor
Role: Vicky Hoffman / Vicky Parker

The Seven Year Itch (1955)
20th Century Fox
Directed By: Billy Wilder
Starring: Tom Ewell
Role: The Girl

Bus Stop (1956)
20th Century Fox
Directed By: Joshua Logan
Starring: Don Murray
Role: Cherie

The Prince and the Showgirl (1957)
Warner Bros.
Directed By: Laurence Olivier
Starring: Laurence Olivier
Role: Elsie Marina

Some Like It Hot (1959)
United Artists
Directed By: Billy Wilder
Starring: Tony Curtis, Jack Lemmon
Role: Sugar Kane Kowalczyk

Let's Make Love (1960)
20th Century Fox
Directed By: George Cukor
Starring: Yves Montand
Role: Amanda Dell

The Misfits (1961)
Seven Arts Productions
Directed By: John Huston
Starring: Clark Gable, Montgomery Clift
Role: Roslyn Taber

Something's Got to Give (1962)
20th Century Fox
Directed By: George Cukor
Starring: Dean Martin, Cyd Charisse
Role: Ellen Wagstaff Arden

ABOUT THE AUTHOR

Jenna Glatzer is the author of seventeen books on topics ranging from health to children's picture books. Recent titles include *Bullyproof Your Child For Life*, which she co-authored with Dr. Joel Haber; *Unbroken*, which she ghostwrote for Tracy Elliott; and the authorized biography *Celine Dion: For Keeps*.

She's also a contributing editor at *Writer's Digest* and has written hundreds of magazine articles. Her home is in New York with her sweet daughter and a patient cat who makes allowances for an overeager toddler.

Visit Jenna at www.jennaglatzer.com.

ACKNOWLEDGMENTS

I dedicate this book to Sarina, the most wonderful baby girl who ever lived.

I also dedicate this book to the memory of two special people who I didn't know, but both of whom sound like the kind of people I wish I had known: "Jiggs" Robison and Ralph L. Roberts.

Thank you first to the people who allowed me to interview them for this book: Angela Allen, Nancy Bacon, Doc Erickson, John Gilmore, Joshua Greene, Diana Hubert, Pat Hopper, Steve Jacobs, John T. Jones, Douglas Kirkland, Kevin McCarthy, Don Obermeyer, Daniel Pinkwater, Don Pond, Robby Robinson, Hal Schaefer, Orven Schanzer, Larry Shaw, Mamie Van Doren, Dicka Wagner, and Paul Wurtzel.

I wouldn't have been able to find a number of those interviewees without the help of some terrific people who put me in contact or shared their notes with me: Mary Susan Britt, Huey Freeman, Lisa Gilman, Enzo Giobbé, Howard Grodske, Corey Levitan, Petri Liukkonen, Frances Lynn, Tim Mangan, Julie Phillips, and Ronald L. Smith.

Thank you also to Michelle Morgan for moral support, and Tony Plant for being my beta reader and a great help in fact-checking. I appreciate the kind photo contribution from Maryanne Murphy and Helen Herrera in memory of their brother, James Murphy. Thank you to Charlie Stuart, Kimmi Richardson, and Ruth Cooke for their helpful feedback and friendship, as well.

Again, the wonderful people at becker&mayer! were terrific to work with. Special thanks to my editor Meghan Cleary, photo researcher Lisa Metzger, and designer Kasey Free for all their help in creating a beautiful book.

And of course, thank you to my family: Lori, Mark, and Paul Glatzer; Lisa and Chris Fries; and my dear Sarina. For, y'know . . . stuff.

IMAGE CREDITS

Every effort has been made to trace copyright holders. If any unintended omissions have been made, becker&mayer! would be pleased to add appropriate acknowledgment in future editions.

Front cover: Michael Ochs Archives/Getty Images
Title page: © Photos 12/ Alamy
Contents page: Allan Grant/Time & Life Pictures/Getty Images
Page 6: Hulton Archive/Getty Images
Page 8: Silver Screen Collection/Hulton Archive/Getty Images
Page 9: Silver Screen Collection/Hulton Archive/Getty Images
Page 10: Hulton Archive/Getty Images
Page 11 (top): Shaan Kokin/Julien's Auctions
Page 11 (bottom): Shaan Kokin/Julien's Auctions
Page 12: Silver Screen Collection/Hulton Archive/Getty Images
Page 13: Silver Screen Collection/Hulton Archive/Getty Images
Page 14: Shaan Kokin/Julien's Auctions
Page 16: Silver Screen Collection/Hulton Archive/Getty Images
Page 17: Shaan Kokin/Julien's Auctions
Page 18: Silver Screen Collection/Hulton Archive/Getty Images
Page 19: Shaan Kokin/Julien's Auctions
Page 20: Courtesy of Don Pond
Page 21: Shaan Kokin/Julien's Auctions
Page 22: Silver Screen Collection/Hulton Archive/Getty Images
Page 23: © Sunset Boulevard/Corbis
Page 24: Silver Screen Collection/Hulton Archive/Getty Images
Page 25: Silver Screen Collection/Hulton Archive/Getty Images
Page 26: Courtesy of David Conover
Page 28: © William Carroll/Corbis
Page 29: The Kobal Collection
Page 30: Content Mine International/Alamy
Page 31: MPTV.net
Page 32: © William Carroll/Corbis
Page 33: © 1978 Richard C. Miller / MPTV.net
Page 34: Silver Screen Collection/Hulton Archive/Getty Images
Page 35: Gene Lester/Getty Images
Page 36: courtesy of Sotheby's/Newsmakers/Getty Images
Page 37 (top): 20th Century Fox/ The Kobal Collection
Page 37 (bottom): © Bettmann/CORBIS
Page 38 (top): 20th Century Fox/ The Kobal Collection
Page 38 (bottom): 20th Century Fox/ The Kobal Collection
Page 39: Courtesy of Diana Markes Levitt
Page 40: © Bettmann/CORBIS
Page 41: © John Springer Collection/CORBIS
Page 42: © Bettmann/CORBIS
Page 43: Michael Ochs Archives/Getty Images
Page 44: The Kobal Collection
Page 45: The Kobal Collection
Page 46: J. R. Eyerman/Life Magazine/Time & Life Pictures/Getty Images
Page 47: © Photos 12/ Alamy
Page 48: © Sunset Boulevard/Corbis
Page 50: Shaan Kokin/Julien's Auctions
Page 51: Hulton Archive/Getty Images
Page 53 (top): 20th Century Fox/ The Kobal Collection
Page 53 (bottom): 20th Century Fox/ The Kobal Collection
Page 54: MGM/ The Kobal Collection
Page 55: MGM/ The Kobal Collection
Page 56: Frank Driggs Collection/Getty Images
Page 57: John Kobal Foundation/Getty Images
Page 58: © Photos 12/Alamy
Page 59: Ed Clark/Time & Life Pictures/Getty Images
Page 60: 20th Century Fox/Getty Images
Page 61: 20th Century Fox/ The Kobal Collection/Frank Powolny
Page 62: 20th Century Fox/ The Kobal Collection
Page 63: © 1978 George E. Joseph / MPTV.net
Page 64: Rex USA
Page 65: MGM/ The Kobal Collection
Page 66: 20th Century Fox/ The Kobal Collection/Bert Reisfeld
Page 68: © Bettmann/CORBIS
Page 69: MPTV.net
Page 70: Shaan Kokin/Julien's Auctions
Page 71: 20th Century Fox/ The Kobal Collection/Bert Reisfeld
Page 72: Rex USA
Page 73: Alfred Eisenstaedt//Time Life Pictures/Getty Images
Page 74: RKO/MPTV.net
Page 75: Silver Screen Collection/Hulton Archive/Getty Images
Page 76: Michael Ochs Archives/Getty Images
Page 77: © Tom Kelley Studios/ Pacific Licensing
Page 78: © Tom Kelley Studios/ Pacific Licensing
Page 79: © Playboy Archive/Corbis
Page 80: MPTV.net
Page 82: MPTV.net
Page 83: Photo File/Getty Images
Page 84: 20th Century Fox/ The Kobal Collection
Page 85: MPTV.net
Page 86: © Sunset Boulevard/Corbis
Page 87: 20th Century Fox/ MPTV.net
Page 88: Generously donated by Scott Fortner of www.MarilynMonroeCollection.com
Page 89: Hulton Archive/Getty Images
Page 90: © CinemaPhoto/Corbis
Page 92: 20th Century Fox/ The Kobal Collection
Page 93 (top): © Bettmann/CORBIS
Page 93 (bottom): MPTV.net
Page 94: Michael Ochs Archives/Getty Images
Page 95: Hulton Archive/Getty Images
Page 96: The Kobal Collection
Page 97: MPTV.net
Page 98: Michael Ochs Archives/Getty Images
Page 99: © 20th Century Fox/ The Kobal Collection
Page 100: Shaan Kokin/Julien's Auctions
Page 102: Popperfoto/Getty Images
Page 103: © Bettmann/CORBIS

Page 104: Michael Ochs Archives/Getty Images
Page 106: Courtesy of Don Obermeyer
Page 107 (top): Courtesy of Don Obermeyer
Page 107 (bottom): Courtesy of Don Obermeyer
Page 108 (top): Courtesy of Don Obermeyer
Page 108 (bottom): Courtesy of Don Obermeyer
Page 109: © Bettmann/CORBIS
Page 110: Gene Lester/Getty Images
Page 111: 20th Century Fox/ MPTV.net
Page 112: © Bettmann/CORBIS
Page 113: 20th Century Fox/ MPTV.net
Page 114 (top): © Bettmann/CORBIS
Page 114 (bottom): © Bettmann/CORBIS
Page 115: © Bettmann/CORBIS
Page 116: © Bettmann/CORBIS
Page 117: AP Photo
Page 118: Michael Ochs Archives/Getty Images
Page 119: Michael Ochs Archives/Getty Images
Page 120: © Michael Ochs Archives/Corbis
Page 121: Hulton Archive/Getty Images
Page 122: The Kobal Collection
Page 123: © Hulton-Deutsch Collection/CORBIS
Page 124: The Kobal Collection
Page 126: © Bettmann/CORBIS
Page 127 (top): Courtesy of Dicka Wagner
Page 127 (bottom): Courtesy of Dicka Wagner
Page 128: Courtesy of Dicka Wagner
Page 129: © Bettmann/CORBIS
Page 130: © Photos 12/Alamy
Page 132: Gene Lester/Getty Images
Page 133: 20th Century Fox/ MPTV.net
Page 134: AP Photo
Page 135: © Bettmann/CORBIS
Page 136: © Bettmann/CORBIS
Page 137: Photographed by Milton H. Greene © 2008 Joshua Greene www.legendslicensing.com
Page 138: Express/Express/Getty Images
Page 139 (top): AP Photo
Page 139 (bottom): © Bettmann/CORBIS
Page 140: © 1978 Sam Shaw/MPTV.net
Page 141: © Bettmann/CORBIS
Page 142: Paul Schutzer/Time & Life Pictures/Getty Images
Page 143 (top): © Photos 12/Alamy
Page 143 (bottom): Content Mine International/Alamy
Page 144: © Bettmann/CORBIS
Page 145: John Bryson//Time Life Pictures/Getty Images
Page 146: Courtesy of Dave Krikac
Page 147 (top): © Bettmann/CORBIS
Page 147 (bottom): Content Mine International/Alamy
Page 148: © 1978 Al St. Hilaire/ MPTV.net
Page 149: © Douglas Kirkland/CORBIS
Page 150: Content Mine International/ Alamy
Page 151: The Kobal Collection
Page 152: Lee Lockwood/Time & Life Pictures/Getty Images
Page 153: © Bettmann/CORBIS
Page 154: © Arnold Newman/Liaison Agency/ Getty Images
Page 156 (top): © Bettmann/CORBIS
Page 156 (bottom): © Bettmann/CORBIS
Page 157: 20th Century Fox/ MPTV.net
Page 158: © CinemaPhoto/Corbis
Page 159: © Arnold Newman/Liaison Agency/ Getty Images
Page 160: © Bettmann/CORBIS
Page 161: Yale Joel/Life Magazine/Time & Life Pictures/Getty Images
Page 162: © Bettmann/CORBIS
Page 163: Hulton Archive/Getty Images
Page 164: © 1978 Ted Allan/ MPTV.net
Page 165 (top): © 1978 Bernie Abramson/ MPTV.net
Page 165 (bottom): © 1978 Bernie Abramson/ MPTV.net
Page 166 (top): © Bettmann/CORBIS
Page 166 (bottom): E. Murray/Fox Photos/Getty Images
Page 168: © Bettmann/CORBIS
Page 169: GABRIEL BOUYS/AFP/Getty Images
Page 170: © Robert Landau/CORBIS
Page 171: Shaan Kokin/Julien's Auctions
Page 172: Keystone/Getty Images
Page 176: © Bettmann/CORBIS

ENVELOPE

Birth certificate: Los Angeles County Registrar
Guardianship paper: Shaan Kokin/Julien's Auctions
Wedding license: Los Angeles County Registrar
Letter to sister: Shaan Kokin/Julien's Auctions
Manager agreement: Shaan Kokin/Julien's Auctions
Magazine: Generously donated by Scott Fortner of www.MarilynMonroeCollection.com
Sketch of Marilyn: © Bettmann/CORBIS
DiMaggio wedding certificate: The City and County of San Francisco, Office of the County Clerk
Wardrobe sketch: Business Wire via Getty Images
Korea tickets: Courtesy of Melinda Mason www.MarilynMonroe.ca
FBI document: AP Photo/FBI
Conversion papers: Courtesy of Christie's Images
Letter to drama coach: © Bettmann/CORBIS
SAG card: Generously donated by Scott Fortner of www.MarilynMonroeCollection.com
Invitation: Generously donated by Scott Fortner of www.MarilynMonroeCollection.com
Painting: Shaan Kokin/Julien's Auctions